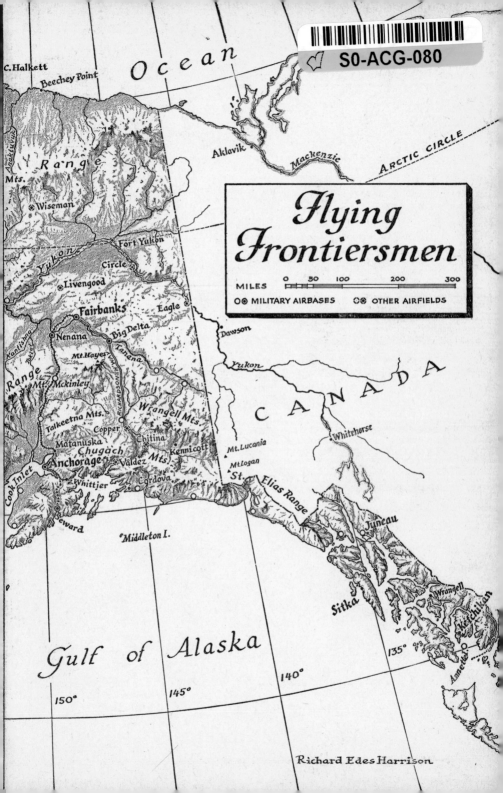

FLYING
FRONTIERSMEN

By Jean Potter

FLYING FRONTIERSMEN

THE MACMILLAN COMPANY
New York, 1956

To
MICHAEL

CONTENTS

PREFACE

These are the true life stories of eight of America's pioneer pilots in the Far North.

I spent a year and a half in Alaska to learn this history, talking and flying with the men who lived it. I owe thanks to many pilots, particularly to Noel Wien and to the late Joe Crosson, survivors of the early period of Alaskan aviation, who patiently told me not only their own stories but also those of fellow-pioneers who had crashed to death.

Wives, mechanics, passengers and friends also helped, for the best flyers are usually silent men, modest men, and others had to remind them of things about their gallant and dangerous work which they themselves forgot.

I am indebted to all those who helped me prepare an earlier book, *The Flying North,* and to those who supplied new material for this book.

I am grateful to the explorer Sir Hubert Wilkins for interviews and for permission to quote from his book *Flying the Arctic* (G. P. Putnam's Sons, New York, 1928); and to Explorer Vilhjalmur Stefansson, to E. L. Bartlett, Alaska's Delegate in Congress, and to C.A.A. Patrol Pilot Jack Jefford for generous assistance. I also thank John Groves of the Air Transport Association and Mrs. Noel Wien for advice on parts of the manuscript.

The endpaper map by Richard Edes Harrison shows Alaska's military and civilian airfields as they were in 1946, at the end of the period during which most of the pioneer "bush" flying was accomplished.

Some of the action described in this book may seem so remarkable that the reader may wonder whether it really took place. I have carefully checked facts with participants and witnesses, or with old records.

This saga of twentieth century frontier history is completely authentic.

FLYING
FRONTIERSMEN

Chapter 1: **OUR ROARING LAST FRONTIER**

Come north with me to our last frontier, Alaska—the land where airplanes are more important than almost anywhere else in the world.

It is the only frontier we Americans have left.

It is an astonishing frontier.

We have found in this Far North country, in the last fifty years, the same challenge of unscaled mountains, unexplored great plain and deep virgin forest as our settlers once found in the Far West.

But the Far North is even more forbidding, and on a grander scale.

Its giant, glaciered snowcaps make the Rockies look tame. Its great plains of tundra are plains such as you have never seen; vast, swampy flats with frozen subsoil, covered by some of the continent's mightiest rivers and by thousands of nameless lakes.

Its tall stand of spruce and hemlock is just beginning to be cut.

The summers of the Far North are warm, but the winters are more hostile than those braved by our western settlers. In the winter Arctic darkness lasts all night and all day, except for a few dim hours around noon. The cold is so intense that low "smoke-fog" hangs above the roofs of wood-burning towns. Oil poured on the snow will freeze so hard that you can handle it like metal. You don't dare run, outdoors, in cold like this, or you may frost your lungs.

We have opened up this challenging frontier mostly in the twentieth century. We have not done it as we once opened up the Far West, first with oxen and covered wagons and then with railroads and roads. As late as 1940, only one long railroad broke the vast wilderness of Alaska, and there were almost no roads.

Airplanes, more than anything else, have opened up the American Far North. And what airplanes!

They were just small, battered, single-engine ships—Swallows or Standards, Stinsons or Pilgrims. They had to be small, slow-landing. As late as 1940 Alaska was a land with almost no real airports.

The foremost frontiersmen of the Far North have been its pilots.

Nothing could stop these rugged young airmen in fur parkas or duck pants and shabby leather jackets. Cramming people and freight into the narrow cabins, they got the planes off the ground somehow, flew them through uncertain skies above the forbidding land and brought them down in the wilds wherever they could.

Even without airports, the Americans in Alaska became probably the flyingest people in the world. Only certain northerly parts of Canada and the Soviet Union may have rivalled their record.

Despite its small population, Alaska flew nearly two thirds as much air freight in 1938 as the entire United States. One of the frontier air strips, during World War II, recorded 10,000 landings and take-offs in a single month—more civilian traffic than La Guardia Field, New York!

Aviation in Alaska has been booming ever since.

A trip over wilderness with one of the "bush" pilots is like no flight that you ever made before.

Minutes after take-off, you gaze out past the wing to a maze of sparsely wooded snow or swamp, confusing as a giant jigsaw puzzle. As the small engine drones on and on you'll look in vain for some sign of life on the earth below. There's not a town in sight, not a farm, not a telephone pole, not a road.

You fly a while like this and you begin to have an odd sensation. You're awed. It's a little as if you were crossing the face of the moon.

The pilot sitting beside you is not awed. This is Main Street, to him. This is his run.

"Bear," he may say, casually, and he'll speed low just over a slope, chasing a terrified grizzly as it lumbers into the brush.

Or "That's Jack Foster's place," he'll tell you, dipping a wing so you can see. He'll probably have to point, before your untrained eyes find the speck of a lone cabin below in the brush.

You start flying into fog. Mist sheets pass the windows. Drops slide down the panes. Soon the "ugly stuff" is rolling all around the plane. You never minded fog when you were a passenger on airliners. You knew that the captain up front was navigating on instruments, following the safe, guiding path of a radio beam.

This is different. The man beside you must fly "contact," navigating by his sight of the earth. Now he has throttled down the engine and you're traveling low, just above the wild marshes, almost as slow as a car. The airspeed indicator reads only eighty miles an hour.

What a way to fly! The earth looks threatening. The scraggly brush below looks almost close enough to touch. A flock of birds lifts, scattering from one of the lonely ponds, just missing the prop. The fog is changing fast. The dark shape of a hill looms just ahead. The plane swerves to avoid it and in the same second that hill is blotted out and another rises beyond.

The pilot sits erect now, working fast. The plane dodges this way and that, trapped in a narrow, shifting channel of murky light.

Then suddenly the pilot jerks the stick back; for a few moments you can't see a thing out of the windows. The small engine roars again at full power. You're spiraling, climbing steeply.

A luminous haze above the plane is getting brighter and brighter. The pilot, sighting the sun dimly through the fog, is using it to escape from the trap you were in down there below. Soon you break out into blue sky above a billowy ocean of unbroken cloud.

You travel a while up there "on top." The cloud mass ahead mounts higher and higher. You're forced to gain altitude. You can't help wishing the plane had more than one engine. You can't help thinking of the small gas tank. You wish your pilot could fly on instruments. You look for a break in the fog and can't find one anywhere. There's no sight of earth but some jagged mountain peaks, sticking up out of the "soup," some distance away.

You can't help worrying how your pilot is going to make it down.

He's whistling. Now he's turning the plane and heading directly toward those jagged peaks. Now he's circling close among them, so close that the rock walls seem to be just a few feet from the wings. You don't like this, as the plane begins to lurch and sink in sudden winds. You wonder if you shouldn't fasten your seat belt, as the pilot keeps circling, turning short, peering down.

Suddenly you see an opening in the fog; thin, flying mists and a glimpse of valley far below—and in that same instant you're jolted violently. He's diving the plane, turning in tight circles, spiraling down.

You'll later learn that this is a famous technique of Alaska's bush pilots when they are trapped on top. They're even warier than most pilots of the gusty air around rough terrain. They know what turbulence can do to their small planes. But they have learned that mountain winds can also be useful, blowing holes in an otherwise unbroken fog. They'll hunt for these risky paths to earth and spiral down through them, dodging sheeting mists, if they must.

You feel by this time that you're flying with a stunt pilot, a daredevil. As you travel low and slow under the fog once more, you've forgotten why the man beside you is maneuvering as he does. When he speaks, he's as matter-of-fact as a bus driver.

"This is Yankee Creek," he tells you. "In a few minutes we'll be landing at Ophir."

The fog is higher here. You look down on the twisted crags of mining country. Then you see a cluster of shacks, and the little scratch that is the runway. The plane circles and bumps down to a stop.

Ophir looks very much like one of the little mine towns of the Far West, with the Stars and Stripes waving from a wooden pole. But there is a difference. This is a town which lives around its airport. The whole population is walking toward your plane as it lands. White men and Indians crowd around the pilot, all talking at once.

"Hi, Jimmy . . . You got my meat? . . . When is Agnes coming over? Thought she'd be with you today . . . You got a package for me from Sears, Roebuck? . . . My radio's on the bum, can you take it now? . . . You need gas? . . . Can you stay to lunch, Jimmy?"

It's like this all over our last frontier. Many roads are now being built in Alaska, but the people of its scattered, remote settlements still depend mostly on planes; small planes on wheels, bumping down on rough clearings and river bars; small planes on skis, making neat parallel tracks as they land in deep snow; small planes on pontoons, sliding down onto the water of lakes or fjords.

The Eskimos, isolated far to the north at the edge of the Arctic Ocean, depend on planes most of all. When the noise of an engine is heard clattering above the shore, people at one of the lone villages begin calling. *"Tingun!* (Machine that flies!)," they cry, in the soft, gentle speech of their people. It echoes all over the village—*"Tingun! Tingun!"* The teacher dismisses school. Everyone walks to meet the landing. Dusky children are so used to planes that they'll swarm on a taxying ship and hop rides, swinging on the struts, standing on the skis.

For a while the Eskimos used aircraft for letter paper. They'd pick out a nice, light-colored ship and scratch on the fabric with knife or pencil:

HELLO FROM THE DIOMEDE PEOPLE

WE GOT TWO WHALES THIS YEAR

OUR PEOPLE ARE ALL WELL

MAYBE I FLY OVER SEE YOU SOON

Messages and replies would travel this way for hundreds of miles. But the scribbling was hard on the fabric. Pilots were annoyed. They asked the Eskimos not to do it. You seldom see it any more.

Today the small planes of the bush pilots share the sky with large aircraft. Today Air Force planes take off from large bases and make routine weather hops to the North Pole. Airliners from the United States speed through Alaska on schedule, heading toward Asia.

During World War II the Army, Navy and Civil Aeronautics Administration built a network of modern airports and airways in the Far North. Pilots flying the mainline can now navigate on instruments, following radio beams. For them trips over Alaska are as routine as trips over the United States.

But the small planes are still flying, and pilots of Alaska are still forced to navigate much of the time bush-style, striking far beyond the mainline to serve the scattered settlements of a frontier that is still new.

The opening up of the Far North by air is history still in the making. The pilots who first pioneered it are not yet old men.

Some of them are still flying, although younger men are now taking the helm.

The Army was startled by Alaska's flying frontiersmen, when it arrived in the north shortly before the war. Military pilots looked down their noses at the shabby planes.

"What kind of a rig is that, old man?" a uniformed Air Force officer asked a rough-clad bush pilot named Bob Reeve. He stared at Reeve's dilapidated red ship with its old-fashioned open radial engine. He hadn't known planes like this flew any more.

"It's a Fairchild," said Reeve, who was lying on the ground underneath it, repairing the tail wheel.

"What model?" asked the officer, disdainfully.

"It's a Fairchild DGA," Reeve told him. "That means Damn Good Airplane! And if you call me an old man again I'll take you over my knee!"

Army flyers didn't look down their noses very long. When emergency airfields had to be hacked from the wilderness, it was the bush pilots who went in with the first freight, landing and taking off without any runways at all.

They knew how to feel for the ground in Arctic winter haze, "dragging" the snowy earth before they landed. Warily touching the snow, on skis, they checked rivers for spider-webbing ice, logs or overflows.

They'd manage take-offs from short clearings where take-off looked impossible, flattening propeller blades for utmost power, using flaps at the last split second for utmost lift and climb. Flying on floats in summer-time, they'd take off from small lakes by circling round and round on the water and then making "step" turns into the wind.

They often cracked up, but they knew cagey ways of "cracking up easy"—knocking off the landing gear as they came down, if necessary, and sliding in "on the belly," or "slipping in" to let one wing absorb the impact.

Accidents did not seem to disturb them. They just repaired their planes and took off again. In Alaska, the Army learned, an airplane "has nine lives—like a cat."

"Spare parts flying in formation," one of the bush pilots grimly said of his ship.

But the Army learned to respect Alaska's air safety record. Despite all the crack-ups, major accidents with loss of life were remarkably few.

"The more I see the bush pilots fly," one military pilot said, "the less I fear an airplane!"

The Army pilots had constant trouble finding their way above the wilderness, before the new airways were built. A compass can't always be trusted over Alaska, because of all the minerals in the ground. And far to the north, above the Arctic Circle, the needle is apt to drift crazily for another reason; because you are flying so close to the earth's magnetic pole.

Army pilots newly arrived from the United States were always getting lost. A Search and Rescue Squadron was formed, but its members spent much of their time searching for each other. Time and again, it was the bush pilots who rescued them.

The bush pilots didn't laugh at the Army. They, too, had lost their way when they first arrived in the Far North. But with time these pioneers had worked out their own way of navigation, developing "contact" flight to a fine art.

They'd learned to take their bearings on wilderness landmarks; the odd form of a hill, the shape of a nameless lake, the special twists of a river. "I know hundreds of lakes," one bush pilot said, "and none of them are on the map." "Two streams," said another, "when you get to know them, don't look no more alike than two people."

One early pilot, flying on pontoons, lost his way in a foggy coastal region, cut by inlets and rivers. Wanting to find out how far inland he was, he landed on the water—and tasted it to see if it were fresh or salt!

The bush pilots had learned to "read" mountain passes, and to follow these twisting gorges in bad weather, flying cautiously at low speed with the stabilizer back—as one described it "almost hanging onto the prop."

"To get through Rainy Pass," a pioneer told a horrified Army pilot, "you start where the Rhon River meets the south fork of the Kuskokwim. There's a cache at the mouth of the creek. Turn left and take the first canyon to your right. You'll see a canyon on your left that looks good, but don't take it. It's blind."

"Take the next left after that and fly up it—it makes a lazy turn to the left, then hard to the right. If you can crawl through under the fog this far you'll make it through. You'll go by a little green lake and come out on Ptarmigan Valley and start down the Happy River past Stillman Lake and then go into Happy River Canyon. . . ."

The Army flyer walked away, shaking his head with awe.

The pilots were all explorers, in the early days. "We discovered the country," one of them says, "because we had to learn to read it—or else."

They helped the United States government make the first reliable maps of the wilderness. They set mapping parties down over and over in the shaggy country and camped out with them while they made their calculations, taking fixes on the stars.

The pilots helped the government survey the Far North's richness of hidden minerals. They flew geologists to the farthest reaches of the Arctic and also landed them over and over in places where human beings had never before set foot.

The pilots even helped to scale some of Alaska's tremendous snowcapped mountains. In 1932, when a scientific party wanted to climb Mt. McKinley, loftiest peak in North America, pilots Joe Crosson and S. E. Robbins flew them to one of its lower slopes and set them down on the tortured, crevassed surface of a glacier, saving them weeks of overland toil.

One of the pioneers, Carl Ben Eielson, ventured still further, striking out from Alaska across the polar sea. He was the first man of any nation to fly a plane across the Arctic Ocean.

The pilots are the most highly respected men on our last frontier, and also the most popular. You can see what they mean to the life of Alaska each summer, when the sun rises high again and the ice crashes down the big rivers and the salmon-fishing season begins. At small seaside villages, float planes circle over the water and slosh down by the wooden canneries, till it seems that they're as thick as the sea gulls.

The pilots wear rubber boots and often carry fishermen and cannery workers piggyback over the mud to shore.

Alaskans remember how the pilots brought whole towns back to life, during the slump that followed the Gold Rush. Big log cabin settlements like Nome and Fairbanks had shrunk to ghost towns, in the nineteen twenties. All the bonanza gold had been dug from nearby ground. Prospectors who wanted to try their

luck further out in the wild country could not haul enough supplies, toiling overland, to last a work season.

The pilots risked their necks to set these men down beside
rich pay dirt, and they hauled their supplies, too.

"If the ship'll take her," they said, "we'll fly her."

Bunks and poling boats were wedged into the small planes.
One of the pilots hauled a dredge shaft in his single-engine Bellanca; he had to take out the front window to fit it in. Another
removed the door of his Stinson to carry a small gas tractor. He
flew it with the track frame sticking out two feet on either
side of the fuselage.

"The tail shook a little," he admitted.

These pilots would and still will fly almost anything to
oblige. Once, when a woman at the town of McGrath needed
fresh milk for her sick baby, Pilot Leo Moore brought her a
cow, in his single-engine Stinson. He reinforced the floor of
the cabin with extra planks, coaxed the animal up a board with
food, roped her head and horns "so she wouldn't take the windows out." But she was calm in flight, he said. She seemed to
like air travel.

In the Far North, if you live in an isolated settlement, your
pilot is your trucker, your grocer, your mailman and your bus
driver, all at once, and that's not all. It may well be that you
owe your life to him; or if you don't, some one of your friends
probably does.

Once a Catholic priest named Father Cunningham was
stricken with pneumonia at a small coastal village named Cape
Prince of Wales. He had a high fever and was sinking fast.
There was no doctor at the Cape.

Pilot Sig Wien flew a short cut out over the open sea to rescue him, in a plane on wheels. The weather was foul, freezing, and Wien's ship dragged heavily under a load of ice. When he arrived at the Cape it was starting to snow. A bad storm was blowing up. Wien bundled the sick priest carefully into the cabin and took off at once. He fought his way back through the blizzard and landed safely at Nome, where Father Cunningham was rushed to a hospital.

The priest lived. Later, when he tried to pay for the trip, Wien just shrugged his shoulders.

There have been countless "mercy flights" in the Far North. A number of babies have been born in the air over Alaska. A pilot knows when women in far-out camps are expecting. He usually flies them to the town hospital in plenty of time. But sometimes the stork fools him.

Pilot Jim Dodson was all alone with a mother in his Stinson when she bore her child. It was an emergency night flight. The plane was roaring through snowfall in the darkness when she kicked the side of the cabin.

"The baby's coming!" she cried.

Luckily Dodson was a calm man, and a husband and father. Controlling the Stinson with one hand, he reached back and did his best to help his passenger with the other. The baby breathed and cried. Dodson radioed for a doctor, who was waiting at the airfield when he landed.

More than one grateful mother-passenger in Alaska has made her pilot her child's godfather.

Nobody needs an airplane like a trapper or prospector in trouble out in the hills. A man alone like this will cut spruce boughs and build an emergency signal in the snow, hoping that a pilot may fly overhead and see it.

HELP

NEED GRUB

HURT

LAND

An Alaska pilot sighting such a signal will risk his neck to come down in the wilds, whatever the risk.

*

Death came to some of the pioneers; sudden, violent death on the snowy tundra, against the jagged, glaciered peaks, in the virgin forest.

Near-disaster was routine for all of them.

Imagine taking off with only a small gas tank, not knowing what kind of weather you will meet, and flying with one engine above the roughest kind of wilderness. Imagine getting lost, or trapped by storm, and having to make a forced landing in the brush "hundreds of miles from nowhere," without any radio to call for help or try to report your position.

Imagine, even if you should reach your destination safely, having to fly low, "dragging" a rough river bar, a shrubbed clearing, a steep hillside, and choose which one to come down on.

Our Far North air pioneers, with time, earned a reputation for being "among the best pilots in the world—because they had to be."

*

Who were they, these "Arctic aces" of Alaska, these flying frontiersmen whose skill and daring have become an international legend?

They were just young fellows from the United States who had to learn their trade the hard way; men from States like Minnesota and North Dakota and Nebraska and California who headed north in this century as their forefathers once headed west.

They came of all walks of life. Ben Eielson was teaching high school and coaching basketball before he took to the northern sky. The distinguished Wien brothers grew up as farm boys. Bob Reeve worked in a newspaper office, Jack Jefford in a jewelers' machinery factory. The uncanny flyer Harold Gillam was operating power shovels before he earned his wings.

It was a common restlessness, the old, driving, democratic, energetic restlessness of America, that took these young men skyward and northward. "We wanted to work in the air," they said, as they told their story, "and flying in the United States was too tame."

They told it tersely, modestly, even reluctantly. They did not want honor for their trail-blazing journeys.

"All in the day's work," they repeated, one after another, shrugging their shoulders.

Perhaps so. But it was some of the most perilous, gallant and hard-fought work that Americans have ever accomplished, in the air or on the ground. Their record is one of which we may all be proud.

Chapter 2: **CARL BEN EIELSON**
Top-of-The-World Lindbergh

Carl Ben Eielson, the founder of aviation in Alaska and the first pilot of any nation to fly a plane across the Arctic Ocean, was a North Dakota boy.

He has been called, and aptly so, America's "top-of-the-world Lindbergh."

A tall young man with a lean face and piercing eyes, Eielson was as modest as Charles Lindbergh, and as daring. In 1928, when he hopped 2,200 miles over the polar sea—from America to Europe—airmen considered his feat as extraordinary as Lindbergh's history-making trans-Atlantic hop the year before. Some experts said it was even more remarkable.

The public, at the time, was less stirred by Eielson's flight. In 1928 most Americans thought of the Arctic as a remote, dreary, useless part of the world. Eielson's name was soon forgotten.

Today it is being spoken again.

As we enter an age of thundering Arctic flight, we are beginning to appreciate what a far-sighted air pioneer he was.

Ben Eielson grew up in the North Dakota town of Hatton, where his father owned a general store and served several terms as mayor. The family lived comfortably in a big, gabled, elm-shaded house. One of nine children, Ben was as active and athletic as most American boys, playing basketball and baseball, swimming and hunting in the out-of-doors. But when he was still very young he showed signs of an unusually curious, serious mind. He spent the evenings of one winter all by himself, studying the Bible.

"You've got to read it," he told his surprised brothers, "if you want to understand history."

He spent the evenings of another boyhood winter poring over Shakespeare.

As a student at North Dakota's University, he was popular, got good marks, made an energetic all-around record. He played varsity sports, joined the debating team, was elected editor-in-chief of the college annual. But he was restless. He switched to another college at the end of his sophomore year. Later he changed colleges again.

Ben Eielson was never content to stay in one place or do one thing very long.

The only thing that held him, throughout his short life, was his passion for aviation.

It was in the Army that he earned his wings, when he enlisted during World War I. After the Armistice, when he was 25, he got himself a small plane, a "Jenny," and launched Hatton's first flying club.

"TIME FLIES!" he advertised in the town paper, in 1920.

"WHEN WILL YOU? TAKE A DIP IN THE CLOUDS! AVIATION IS COMING INTO ITS OWN! The men who thought aviation was dangerous a year ago are taking rides today. Many men who think it is dangerous today will be owning ships in five years. We are approaching an AERIAL AGE!"

His father was violently opposed to all this. Certain that Ben would be killed, he threatened more than once to burn his Jenny.

We smile to think that aviation was considered dangerous in the United States such a short time ago.

But when Ben Eielson soloed, the Army had a magnificent total of only 35 trained pilots—all told!

In the early nineteen twenties pilots were considered a reckless lot, pretty much in a class with circus daredevils.

It was not long before Ben wrecked his Jenny, tangling with telephone wires as he tried to take off from a cow pasture. His father persuaded him to go back to college to study law. Nobody was surprised when he slammed his lawbooks shut a few months later and announced that he was heading north to Fairbanks, Alaska, to take a job teaching high school. It was just like Ben to roam to a faraway land. In a way, the family was relieved.

"At least," his father told his brothers and sisters, "there are no airplanes up there."

But as Ben Eielson traveled to Alaska aboard a small steamer in the fall of 1922, his thoughts were not those of a school teacher.

As the rough train of Alaska's one and only railroad rocked him slowly north toward the town of Fairbanks, he gazed out the window with awe.

What a country! What a country for planes!

The locomotive was drawing its creaking load past snowcaps loftier than any he had ever seen. Most of these mountains had never been climbed or even named, as yet. This was really a frontier. The railroad was still being built; at one place passengers had to get off and hike to another rail-head.

It was a long journey. The second day, as the train chugged north toward the Arctic Circle, the peaks sank down into a vast, empty plain. The autumn flats seemed to roll on endlessly. Eielson was startled when at last the bustling log cabin town of Fairbanks loomed up ahead at the end of the line.

A town seemed lost in this wilderness, as lost as a ship at sea. Most of the frontier settlements, he knew, were not as lucky as Fairbanks. They were not even on the railroad. Their streets stopped short at town limits, with no roads beyond. The only way a man could move between them was a slow way; on foot, or by river boat in summer, in winter by dog team.

Eielson was full of ideas. Planes could bring the settlements close. Planes could change all of life in this country!

He took a small room in an old Gold Rush hotel and reported for his job at the red frame high school, teaching math and general science and coaching basketball. Soon he was the most popular teacher the school had ever had. As often as not, he would forget the day's lesson. Pupils listened with fascination as he told them about aviation, the tough things about it and the great things about it and what it could mean in a vast, roadless land like theirs.

Alaska, he also told them, had a big future in terms of international flying. He pointed out that it lay on the shortest, most direct route between the United States and the Orient. Silks, mail and other light freight would soon speed through the Far North by air, he said, instead of rocking slowly across the mid-Pacific by boat. Before many years Fairbanks would be a cross-roads city of the world.

"I came up here to teach," he said, "but what I really want to do is fly."

Now and then Eielson would turn and gaze out the schoolroom window in silence. Sometimes, deep in thought, he seemed to be looking nowhere. Other times he stared over the roofs at the town ball park, where a group of Army flyers from the United States, the Black Wolf Squadron, had landed two years before.

He liked to talk about the Squadron and the daring flight it had made, hedge-hopping all the way north from the United States through the wilds of Canada in four open-cockpit De Havillands, and then hedge-hopping all the way back. They'd cracked up many times en route, but they'd made it. And now other pilots were arriving in the north, he told his pupils. That very summer, a few months before his own arrival, a boy from Buffalo, Clarence Prest, had brought a plane to southeastern Alaska by steamer and flown it there till he'd smashed it in a swamp. And a fellow named Roy Jones had flown a Curtiss flying boat all the way from Seattle and was now basing at a southeast fishing town. But there were no planes yet in all of inland and Arctic Alaska.

"I want a ship!" Eielson said. "If this town will buy me a ship, I will show what can be done."

He talked aviation everywhere he went; under the stuffed mooseheads of the hotel lobby; in the dingy frontier newspaper

CARL BEN EIELSON: Top-of-The-World Lindbergh

JOE CROSSON: The Gallant Flyer

NOEL WIEN: The Cautious Dean

HAROLD GILLAM: Ace of Storms

BOB REEVE: Bird of the Glaciers

ARCHIE FERGUSON: The Flying Clown

FRED MOLLER: The Little Giant

JACK JEFFORD: Builder of the Airways

office; in the false front cafes and mining supply stores up and down the unpaved main street.

Some people said the new school-teacher was a dreamer, the impractical kind. Yet his sharp eyes had the look of a man of action. One thing was certain; everyone liked him. Like many of the town's merchants and miners, he was of Scandinavian descent—"as stubborn a Norwegian as you could find." He was keen and friendly and warm. Soft-spoken, he argued earnestly. Boyishly confident, he never swaggered. Guests crowded around him at parties. Schoolboys began to follow him through the streets like hound-dogs.

He had been teaching school only a few months when he wrote a letter to one of his brothers back in Hatton; "The City Council has offered to put up a thousand dollars toward getting a plane. Do not mention this to Dad, as I am not sure yet, anyhow, and it would worry him."

The merchants came through, and Fairbanks' first plane, a Jenny, arrived crated in the railroad freight car the following summer. Eielson towed it to the ball park—the best thing around for an airfield. The park's bleachers were black with curious people as he took off on July 3, 1923, for his first flight in the Far North.

He later laughed at himself, remembering this historic journey. In the United States it would have been an easy hop. He planned to fly only fifty miles, to a small settlement called Nenana. He could have followed the railroad all the way.

But he was too new in the north to be wary of the wilderness. He left the track and started flying cross-country. Before long he had to admit he was lost.

Lost? How could he be lost so close to Fairbanks? Where was Nenana? Where was the railroad? The strange rolling wilds below all looked the same.

He flew around for some time before he found the dark line of the track again. This time he was careful to follow it to his destination. He gave a stunting exhibition at Nenana—and earned half the cost of his new Jenny in one day.

But stunting did not interest Eielson. That summer he made good his promise to Fairbanks, hopping passengers to outlying settlements, cutting their travel time from hard-fought days to easy hours or minutes. The town was overwhelmed by this fast new means of transport. Eielson, however, was already restless, discontent with his Jenny. What was a range of 150 miles, he asked, in a land like Alaska? That was all the small ship had.

New plans were stirring in his mind. One day he sat down and wrote a letter to Washington, offering to fly the United States mail in the Far North and asking the Post Office Department to send him a longer-range plane.

There was no answer. His friends told him that he would never have an answer. They laughed at his nerve in writing to Washington. He kept on writing letters.

"Ben was hitting over our heads," the mayor of Fairbanks remembers. "He was born to something bigger than we realized."

One day that fall the town paper, the *News-Miner,* hit the streets with a big banner headline: MAIL SERVICE FOR KUSKOKWIM THROUGH AIR.

Townsfolk were much impressed as they read the details. The Post Office Department in Washington was shipping the young school-teacher-flyer an official government plane, a De

Havilland powered by a Liberty engine. Eielson was expected to make ten mail flights to a town called McGrath, far out in the wild Kuskokwim River country, all of 300 miles away.

The government, the newspaper announced, was not at all sure that Eielson would succeed. The flights were considered experimental. People were surprised by the low pay that he was to draw for such dangerous work; only two dollars a mile, less than half what it cost the government to deliver the mail by dog team.

Eielson was not thinking about money. Delighted, he prepared for his venture into the unknown. It was just this, for the first mail flights were to be made in wintertime.

No plane had ever been flown in winter in Alaska.

It is difficult for us today to appreciate what this meant. Back in 1925 nobody in America knew whether or not aircraft could operate safely in the extreme low temperatures of the Far North. Some experts declared that the oil and fuel would certainly freeze. The engine would quit, they insisted, if you could ever get it started. They said that ice would form on the wings in flight, dragging the ship to earth.

If Eielson was worried, he did not show any sign of it. He said that he was sure that a plane could fly in Alaska in winter. He was only impatient to prove it.

His friends shook their heads when his new De Havilland arrived by boat and rail from Washington. It was on wheels! How could it land and take off in the snow? The Post Office Department was crazy, people said. The ship might be all right for the United States, but not for Alaska.

Eielson calmly removed the wheels and asked a local carpenter to build a pair of skis. The man was very nervous about the responsibility of making skis for an airplane. How long should they be? How heavy? There were many arguments. He finally turned out a big, flat-bottomed pair of hickory. They weighed 300 pounds; much more than later pilots were to find best for safe and effective use.

Eielson's first, history-making mail flight was made on February 21, 1924. The sun rose late in the morning, as it always does at Fairbanks at that time of year. The bitter cold air was hazy above the white land. In the hours before flight time Eielson and his helpers went to the ball park in the darkness. They warmed the plane as best they could, in its flimsy wooden hangar, by means of old-fashioned stoves. They heated the oil.

Stamping their feet and beating their hands, the Fairbanks crowd watched suspensefully as the De Havilland was pulled out onto the snow. The United States mail—500 pounds of it—was hastily loaded aboard. Eielson, bundled heavily in furs and wearing a long pair of black bearskin mittens, climbed alone into the open cockpit. People wondered how he was going to endure the cruel blast as he went whistling in this open rig through the sky.

Onlookers stood tense and silent as he revved up the engine, tested it a long time.

They watched him taxi along in the snow to the end of the short park.

The engine roared loud in the stillness. Eielson smiled, waved a mittened hand. There were cheers as the De Havilland rushed ahead on its clumsy skis and lifted, trailing whiteness, into the sky.

During the first critical minutes, as he gained altitude, Eielson listened to his engine as he had never listened to an engine before. It was running smoothly.

As he sped alone through the sub-Arctic haze, he watched the wings for signs of forming ice. There were none.

He found the dog-trail that led to McGrath and began to follow it. Weather permitting, he planned to follow it the whole way. "Keep to the trail!" his friends had warned him. "That's no place for a man to get lost in winter, out there in the Kuskokwim country."

Should he lose his way and make an emergency landing somewhere off-trail, they'd warned him, he might not be found by search parties for days, weeks—maybe even months. Men struggling over the vast, rolling swamplands in the snow, on foot or by dog team, would have no idea where to look for him. He would freeze or starve to death, even if he hadn't been hurt in the crash.

"Keep to the trail!" It was an easy thing to say. Eielson had a constant, wary eye on the sky ahead. His only weather report had been from McGrath itself, telegraphed by relay to Fairbanks, and it was already out of date. How could he keep to the trail if he should run into a blizzard, or even a local snow flurry? Sudden fog, rolling toward him over the flats, could snatch away his sight of the thin, trampled path below and he might not be able to find it again.

Luckily, the sky did not change.

Once he spied some black specks crawling on the white expanse below: a driver with his dog team. He flew down with a flourish to salute the man. It was a great moment. Twenty days of hard work, it took the fellow to make the mail run to McGrath, stopping at roadhouses all along the way.

With luck, the De Havilland was going to make it to Mc-Grath and back to Fairbanks again the same day!

Right on schedule, Eielson sighted the roofs of McGrath and a crowd of people running out of their cabins. He landed smoothly in the snow. The first winter mail flight had been made all the way with no trouble at all.

But the return flight to Fairbanks came close to being the last flight of Eielson's life.

Knowing the shortness of the Far North winter day, he had planned to stop at McGrath only long enough to exchange the mails. The excited crowd begged him to stay longer. They had prepared a big banquet in his honor. He felt he couldn't disappoint them. It was two o'clock in the afternoon before he took off, and he knew that he had barely time to reach his home base by dark.

Or would there be time enough? The sky was already dimmer than he'd figured. He had not been long in the air when he was forced to a grave decision. It was too late for him to follow the dog trail back. He would have to leave the trail and take a shorter route, striking out over unknown wilds, navigating the best he could by compass.

For nearly two hours the plane soared like a lone bird above the earth in the deepening dusk. The cold grew more and more intense, as the sun sank. The engine was still running smoothly, but the compass route did not take Eielson where he had expected. He scanned the wilds for landmarks. There were none. There was nothing, nothing at all, to show that human beings had ever set foot in the desolate-looking, frozen swamps below him.

He began to fly in circles. He had to admit to himself that he was lost.

Sighting a big river, he decided to follow it. He knew that much of the frontier's population was scattered along the waterways. But there was no sign of life along the banks. He did not even know what river it was, nor did he know in what direction its twisting course was leading him. The bends came so fast that his compass had no time to settle down to a heading.

By this time it was dark. The sky was overcast; there was not a star showing. His plight was critical.

Any pilot knows how dangerous it is to fly "contact" over strange country at night. Only a fool or a man in desperation would do it. The land that slid beneath the De Havilland's wings looked flat, as well as he could make it out. But he could see nothing ahead in the pitch-blackness, and he knew that he had been flying around long enough to be approaching mountains.

There was nothing to do but head blindly on, trying to follow the river below. He continued this course for another hour. His gas supply was getting low when he saw a flicker of light in the distance. But as he cut his altitude and approached he saw that it was no town, just a single, faint beam, probably cast by the oil lamp of a lone trapper's cabin.

He circled above it, debating. Should he make a crash landing here in the brush, in the dark? Here there was a human being. Here there was warmth, shelter. Later, if his gas ran out before he found a town, he would have to crash-land just as blind and all alone in the snowy swamp or forest.

He was tempted, but the thought of wrecking his new government plane held him back. He decided to take the long chance of finding Fairbanks and stay in the air as long as he could.

He managed to find the river again, and followed it once more, now perilously low, just over the tree-tops. Even at this altitude, his smarting eyes could barely make out the dark, timbered line of the banks against the snow.

The gas was almost gone when he saw another flicker of light, far ahead in the gloom.

This time, as he approached, he looked down to a strange and welcome sight; several bonfires, burning around what seemed to be some sort of clearing. He was puzzled. What place might this be? Whatever it was, he would have to take a chance on it.

Bracing himself, he began to cut altitude.

As he got close, the murky earth began to take shape in the flicker of the fires. Too late, he saw a flash of treetops just ahead of the plane.

The De Havilland shivered and there was a rending crash as one of the wings struck branches.

Then he was upside down in the cockpit, as the plane rolled violently over on its back.

"Ben! Ben! By golly, he made it!"

Stunned, he heard the voices, saw the faces of his friends around him. This was Fairbanks! This was his home base!

The crowd that came spilling into the ball park from town was wild with excitement. They'd hardly been able to believe it when they'd heard the sound of his engine in the night sky. It had been so late that most people had gone home, giving him up for lost. Only a few men had stayed at the park, hoping against hope, refusing to let the fires go out.

Eielson was not hurt in the crash. Hoisted onto a friend's shoulders, the exhausted flyer was carried in triumph into the hangar, where the mayor, on behalf of all the people in town, presented him with a gold watch. There were shouts for a speech.

He was much too dazed from his long ordeal to address the crowd.

"The plane," he kept asking, over and over, "what's the damage to the plane?"

The landing gear and one ski had been broken, and the propeller damaged. But in the days that followed local mechanics helped him repair them.

He continued the mail flights as scheduled.

Each time he took off from his home base he seemed calm. His smile was unfailing as he waved to the crowd. But his narrow escape from death that night had affected him more than most people knew. He admitted to a friend that he lay awake before some of the mail trips all night long. Other nights, to the alarm of people in his hotel, he rose and prowled in his sleep. Once a neighbor found him wrestling with the foot of his bed. "I'm trying to set the tail!" he shouted. "But the darn wind keeps changing!" Another time he was trying to jump out the upper-floor window, and fought off rescuers so violently that they had to knock him out. After this disturbing event his landlady moved him to the ground floor.

Eielson's friends worried about these signs of tension. Somebody said that he didn't seem to be the swash-buckling, devil-may-care aviator type. This was true. Those who knew him well report that flying did not come easy to him. He was less a "natural-born pilot"—as compared with some of Alaska's other airmen—than a pilot of remarkable imagination. He was driven to make his dangerous, trail-blazing journeys because he was determined to show what planes could mean.

Carrying the mail was not enough. He did everything he could think of to dramatize the advantage of air transport over transport by dog teams. Asking for copies of the town paper just off the press, he dropped them by means of small, bright-colored parachutes to roadhouses along his route. Once he rushed a bale of needed wire to an outlying telegraph station. He always welcomed emergency freight.

These were days of glad accomplishment for Eielson. So moved were the Indians at McGrath by his new service that they initiated him into their tribe. "Moose Ptarmigan Ben," they called him. It was a rare honor for a white man. But the spring thaw brought new danger. One day as Eielson landed at McGrath the skis tore through the river ice and were broken off. He decided that it was time for him to put the government's plane back on wheels. After this he used a river bar for his McGrath landings. Springtime wheel landings on the Fairbanks ball park, however, presented more of a problem.

The park, only 1,400 feet long, with stumps and a high wood-pile at one end, had been a poor enough runway even for ski-landings in winter. Warming weather now made a soggy soup of it, with a trench of water bordering the runway. The wheeled De Havilland, sloshing down onto the mud at sixty miles an hour, cracked up time after time.

One day Eielson brought a passenger into Fairbanks, a sick

Swede who needed hospital care. The plane ploughed down on the park and crashed over on its back. Eielson, in his excitement, released his passenger's safety belt and the man fell on his head.

"Gosh, Ben!" he muttered. "You always land like this?"

Eielson grinned, sheepish.

"Well—not *always!*"

The eighth mail flight was fated to be the last one. This time the plane crashed sideways on the Fairbanks field. The propeller, the rudder and two of the wing struts were badly damaged. Local mechanics could not repair them without new parts from the United States.

Eielson telegraphed Washington about this accident, asking the Post Office Department to ship the needed parts. The reply was a shock. The government not only refused to send the parts, but also ordered the plane shipped back by boat to the United States. "Your experiment," the Assistant Postmaster General wrote Eielson, "has been successful to a marked degree." The rest of his letter was double-talk. It was plain to see that Washington officials considered Alaskan air mail much too risky.

Eielson left Alaska that summer and went to Washington to argue his case. Once again he was full of new plans, bigger plans this time than pioneer flights inside Alaska itself. He was talking about flying out over the polar sea beyond. He said he was sure that with the right equipment he could fly over the North Pole. "Easy!" he told his friends.

"Never satisfied to take it slow," says the mayor of Fairbanks. "Always restless, aiming higher and higher. That was the key to Ben."

Eielson badgered the Post Office Department and also haunted the offices of Army chiefs.

"The short way to fly to Europe or Asia," he quietly told them, "is over the north. All we have to do is look at a globe."

Conventional Army officers of the day did not know what to make of this persistent young flyer with his outlandish ideas. When he suggested that the Army should pioneer an air route through Alaska to the Orient, they curtly told him that they did not have adequate planes. Rebuffed by lesser men, he finally got an interview with General Billy Mitchell. The far-sighted General encouraged him. Mitchell shared Eielson's vision of the Arctic as the aerial crossroads of the future. But both men were a quarter of a century ahead of their time.

The year 1925 went badly for Eielson. There was no action from the War Department. He bid against the dog teams for Alaskan mail transport, but the Post Office Department chose the dogs. He tried to persuade a large New York aviation company to put money into Alaska. Executives coldly told him that it would be a losing proposition.

He managed to get a temporary Army assignment at Langley Field, Virginia, where he spent several months studying navigation and night-flying techniques and helping to perfect an airplane ski for winter operation. When this ended, he went back to his home town with scarcely a cent in his pockets.

His father begged him to forget his "flying craze" and go into business with a brother, Oliver, as a bond salesman. He finally agreed.

"Ben didn't like it at all," Oliver remembers. "He was depressed as the dickens. But we persuaded him he should make some easy money for a while."

Luckily for America's record in the Arctic, Ben Eielson did not have to spend his time selling bonds very long.

It was an explorer who rescued him from this fate. In several nations, men who had ventured over the Arctic Ocean by sledge or on foot were talking of trying to conquer the little-known region by air.

One day, as Eielson was sitting moodily in a barber shop while on a business trip, he got a phone call from his father. The news was electrifying: the famous dean of Arctic explorers, Vilhjalmur Stefansson, was trying to reach him. Stefansson was helping his friend, the Australian explorer-flyer Captain George Wilkins, organize an expedition out over the Arctic Ocean north of Alaska. Wilkins was looking for pilots, and Stefansson wondered whether Eielson would be interested in a job.

Ignoring the pleas of his anxious father and brothers, he left the very next night to talk with the two explorers in New York. Stefansson and Wilkins warned him that the expedition had limited funds and would not be able to pay him much. He hardly heard them. He was in a mood to make the flights for nothing. He signed up at once, at a small salary, for the extreme peril of polar work.

Chapter 3: EIELSON OVER THE ARCTIC

In 1926, only three years after he had made his first Alaska flights in a Jenny, Eielson returned to Fairbanks planning to fly across the top of the world.

By this time other flyers were basing at Fairbanks, carrying on the work he had begun. The town had built a better airfield and was getting used to planes. But Fairbanksans had never seen the like of the Wilkins expedition. There were two Fokkers, one of them a large tri-motor. Eielson was one of several pilots, including an imposing Army major who had been commandant of a pursuit squadron. Reporters and photographers had also arrived to cover the big air event.

The expedition's projects stunned everyone at the log cabin town. Wilkins announced that he planned to fly 500 miles to the very top of the continent, and set up a base at an ice-locked, wind-swept settlement called Barrow. Then he proposed to fly out over the frozen sea to explore for unknown islands. Finally, he said he was going to fly all the way across the Arctic Ocean to Europe!

A large crowd gathered at the airfield to watch the planes christened with wine at a "launching" ceremony. There was much cheering. But the expedition got off to a bad start, a start that seemed an evil omen of things to come.

As the Army major taxied out in the three-engine Fokker, it swerved into a snow-drift and the whirling prop cut off the head of a reporter who was standing beside the runway.

The next day, as Eielson flight-tested the second plane, he stalled it. It ploughed into a fence and the prop and under-carriage were damaged.

Eielson's old friends were much disturbed. Remarks were heard that he did not have much experience with planes of this size. But when the imposing Army major took the tri-motor off the ground for the first time he, too, stalled and crashed, with even greater damage.

Fairbanks began to ridicule Wilkins. People said there was a jinx on the expedition. Now Eielson's friends took him aside and warned him to quit while the quitting was good. Hadn't he had enough narrow escapes on the mail flights? What would happen if he tried to cross the polar sea? They said it would be suicide.

Eielson laughed. Already, he was Wilkins' firmest supporter. He respected his chief's long record as an Arctic explorer and navigator. He was no more discouraged by the setbacks than was Wilkins himself. Although Eielson had less experience as a pilot than some of the others attached to the expedition, it was he who was to be at the controls of Wilkins' planes during most of the daring journeys of the next few years.

Impatient to begin the first task of freighting fuel and supplies to the Barrow base, Wilkins and Eielson surveyed the two wrecked Fokkers. The tri-motor was too damaged for use. The second plane, however, looked as if it could be safely flown with a new propeller. Wilkins decided to buy an old Club prop from a local pilot rather than wait for a better one to be shipped from the United States.

The Fairbanks crowd watched with nothing less than horror as Eielson and Wilkins climbed into the single-engine plane with the makeshift prop and took off on the first flight in history ever made to Barrow. The two men had not even been able to find out what the weather was at the god-forsaken town at the top of the continent! There was no telegraph station there. Barrow, 500 miles to the north, was almost as far from Fairbanks as Alaska was from the United States! How would Eielson find his way, even in good weather? The country that he must cross was the wildest, least-known, most forbidding part of all Alaska. Few white men had ever been into the region, even on foot or by dog team.

It was indeed a dangerous venture.

It is difficult for anyone who has not flown the route from Fairbanks to Barrow to appreciate the nerve that it took to make the first air journey.

Even today the flight is one of the most awesome in the world. Two hundred miles north of Fairbanks the mysterious Endicott Mountains, "jaggedest on the continent," tower steeply from the Arctic plain. The pilot of a single-engine plane must fly through these mountains for 150 miles, finding his way in a maze of dizzying canyons between the savage peaks. There is an almost frightening splendor to this Arctic extravagance of the earth. Even the pilots of modern transports, crossing the range at altitude, have reported a sensation of gloom.

Then there is an immensity of empty tundra country to be crossed. And when a flyer reaches the top of the continent, finding Barrow, the farthest-north town under the American flag, is a challenge. During World War II an Army pilot who had radio contact with the isolated settlement flew 500 purposeful miles north from Fairbanks and 500 angry miles back. "There's no damn town up there!" he said. "Nothing but snow and ice!"

Eielson had never made a flight like this one. He and Wilkins had only their unreliable compass and a map to guide them, and when they reached the Endicott Mountains they discovered that the map, the best available in that year, was hardly worth the paper it was printed on.

"What's the altitude of these peaks?" Eielson asked Wilkins.

"They're marked at 5,000 feet here," Wilkins replied, frowning.

The giant snowcaps ahead towered into the sky to an altitude of at least 10,000!

It was like a nightmare, as their plane roared through the unknown canyons. But they managed to find a way across the Arctic Divide. Then the timber line of the continent sank behind them, and they started out over the flat, treeless, snowy tundra country beyond. Even to an experienced explorer like Wilkins, it was awesome. "Weird and uncanny," he later described it.* "The monotony and uncertainty of it would drive any man crazy if endured for long."

---

* A number of the Wilkins quotations in this book are taken from his book *Flying the Arctic*, courtesy of G. P. Putnam's Sons, New York.

At last their watches told them that they should be reaching the top of America. They scanned the frozen expanse below in vain. Finally Wilkins realized, from the structure of the pressure ridges, that sea ice lay below. He and Eielson had not only missed Barrow; the snowy land and sea had appeared so much the same that they had passed the coast altogether without knowing it. They were now heading out over the Arctic Ocean.

Wilkins was in no mood to turn back. Knowing that the Fokker still had gas to spare, he decided to give Eielson a surprise and put him to a test. He let him continue unknowing for another hour. Then he passed him a note through the aperture of the dual-control plane; "If you look ahead you will see 100 miles farther north in this area than any man has seen from the air until today. What do you say to going on another half hour, just for good measure?"

Eielson was learning what a dauntless explorer his chief was. Many a pilot would have objected that finding Barrow could be difficult enough, before the fuel ran out.

He smiled. "Whatever you think best," he replied.

When they finally turned back toward land, a blizzard was blowing up over the ice. They searched for Barrow until it seemed hopeless. They were plagued by mirages. Houses and villages seemed to rise up everywhere, dim in the flying snow, till at last they sighted a coastal bluff, followed the edge of the land around and Eielson landed the Fokker smoothly on the Barrow lagoon.

Several more freighting trips were made to the Barrow base that summer, laying in fuel and supplies. Forced to make one plane do instead of two, Eielson and Wilkins carried a heavier load each time. On the last trip the single-engine Fokker lumbered through the Endicotts with 4,750 pounds aboard—more than twice the weight it had been designed to haul.

Slowed by mechanical trouble and fog, the expedition was unable to make any more flights out over the ice pack in 1926. Arctic publicity of the year went to Explorer Richard Byrd, who flew from Spitsbergen to the Pole and back, and to the crew of the dirigible *Norge,* which flew from Spitsbergen to Alaska. But Eielson and Wilkins delivered enough fuel to Barrow for extensive Arctic work. They went back to the United States that winter and the expedition returned north the next year with two Wright-powered Stinson biplanes.

On the morning of March 29, 1927, they left Barrow on their first long flight out over the Arctic Ocean.

The weather was fair, the temperature 30 below zero. The explorer and his pilot were in high spirits. As their plane sped out farther and farther over the glittering pack, Wilkins began the expedition's real work, taking valuable notes on ice conditions and scanning the frozen sea for possible unknown land. He hoped to discover an island north of the continent on which a weather station could be built.

They were five and a half hours out from Barrow, hovering alone above the vast, white expanse, when they heard a dread sound.

The engine began to miss. It was missing too badly to stay in the air. They would have to land!

In a split second, Eielson wondered; could a wheeled plane come down safely out here on the moving pack ice?

He knew that explorers had been debating the question. Wilkins thought such landings should be possible. Others disagreed. Nobody had ever tried.

There was no time for debate now.

He put the Stinson into a long, slow glide and headed for the smoothest-looking stretch of pack ice that he and Wilkins could see within range.

The wheels touched. The plane bumped to a rough but safe stop.

Wilkins was too impressed by this history-making landing on the pack ice to worry about their predicament. As Eielson anxiously revved up the faulty engine, he leapt out of the plane and began taking echo-soundings to measure the depth of the Arctic Ocean below. But the roar of the engine interfered with his work. He asked Eielson to turn it off.

Eielson hesitated. He later told his chief what his thoughts had been: "Go ahead and take the sounding. If we stop the engine we will never get it started again, and nobody but you and me will ever know what the sounding is."

Cheerfully, without a word, he cut the engine.

Wilkins found that there were more than three miles of water under the ice—the greatest depth that had ever been registered in the Arctic Ocean. But this contribution to science was to cost him and his game pilot a bitter experience.

Eielson had to work two hours in the 30-below-zero cold before he had the engine running again. By this time an ugly storm was brewing. He managed to take off, after four unsuccessful tries. But the plane had been aloft only ten minutes when the engine missed again. Once more he made a safe emergency landing on the ice. The plane shuddered in gusty wind and snow began to fill the sky as he worked still another hour over the engine. When he took off again it was into a howling blizzard, and night was falling.

It was soon so dark that Eielson could no longer see the compass and turn-and-bank indicator in the unlighted cockpit. Wilkins had to lean over the gas tank with a guarded torch-light and guide him by touching him on the arm.

They flew a long way like this, "crabbing" in the direction of Barrow against a forty-mile side-wind. This, and the many false tries at take-off had brought their fuel supply perilously low. Suddenly, without any warning, the roar of the engine sputtered down into silence. Eielson snapped the switch right and left with no response.

This time the engine was dead, and they would have to land at once *in the dark* on the rough-ridged, frozen sea below.

"We could feel the sag of the falling plane," Wilkins remembers. "With great coolness and skill, Eielson steadied the machine, righting her to an even keel and a steady glide. . . . As we came to within a hundred feet of the ground . . . we could dimly see it serrated with ice ridges, but we had no idea of height or distance.

"Near the ground the air was rough. The plane swerved and pitched but Eielson, still calm and cool, corrected the controls for each unsteady move. In a moment we were in the snow-drift. We could not see beyond the windows of the plane. I felt Ben brace himself against the empty gas tank. I leaned with my back against the partition wall of the cabin and waited.

"The left wing and the skis struck simultaneously . . . I gripped Eielson's shoulder and slipped through the door of the machine. Wind and driving snow filled my eyes. Dimly about us I saw pressure ridges as high as the machine. We had undoubtedly struck one as we came down. . . . The machine still rested on the skis, but they had turned on their sides, the stanchions twisted and broken."

They were marooned on an island of ice. Wilkins figured that they were about sixty-five miles northwest of Barrow, drifting slowly toward the east at a speed of several miles an hour.

The blizzard howled down for five days as they huddled helpless in their damaged Stinson. At last, on the sixth day, the storm broke. The weather was colder, and clear. Wilkins calculated that the ice island had by this time been driven along parallel to the coast to a point about a hundred miles northeast of the northernmost town.

The two men knew that their only chance of survival would be to leave the shelter of their plane and start walking back to America across the pack ice.

They hastily built make-shift sleds from part of the plane's cowling and a tail ski, and loaded them with emergency supplies from the cabin. Draining what little fuel was left in the tank, they rigged up a burner from a gallon can. Then they abandoned their plane and began, on foot, the long trek toward land.

For thirteen days they fought their way, sinking to their waists in soft drifts, crawling on their hands and knees across broken pressure ridges, wrenching their feet and ankles as they pulled themselves between walls of steel-like ice, slipping and falling and getting up again.

Wilkins showed Eielson how to use the snow to live by, melting it for drinking water and building shelters of it, Eskimo-style, to sleep in. Guided by so experienced an explorer, Eielson was in no danger of freezing, despite the cold. But he was suffering constant pain. During his repeated work on the engine, he had forgotten to keep his hands covered, and as a result he had frozen several fingers. His hands were so blistered and blackened that he could not use them. He hauled his share of the supplies by means of his armpits.

Not once, Wilkins later reported, did he complain.

On the morning of April 16 they sighted land at last and stumbled up to a fur-trading station called Beechey Point, 180 miles to the east of Barrow. The people there could hardly believe their eyes. They were half afraid of the two haggard men who appeared on foot out of the vast reaches of the mysterious, frozen sea, with so unlikely a story.

Once more the two pioneers had made history. They had proved that men marooned far out on the polar ice pack can walk with safety to land.

Eielson was to have a further ordeal, and a grim reminder of the adventure for the rest of his life. As soon as he and Wilkins, rescued by another pilot, reached Barrow, it was necessary for the local missionary to amputate the little finger of his right hand. There was no doctor at Barrow to perform the operation.

He sent his family in North Dakota a snapshot of his extraordinary arrival at the top of the continent. The picture showed him standing on the ice in his fur parka, his face, blackened by exposure, alight with a gay smile. The note scrawled on the back gave no hint of what he had accomplished and endured. "After a walk on the Arctic Ocean," it said. That was all.

Wilkins and Eielson returned to the United States that fall to buy a specially equipped Lockheed Vega and in 1928 returned once more to Barrow, determined to make the first airplane hop across the Arctic Ocean, from Barrow to Spitsbergen.

Their small, single-engine monoplane was relatively untried, the second of the kind ever built. It had two extra gas tanks in each wing for the long journey, and a novel window had been built into the floor to give Wilkins vertical vision. The ship also had, for that year, an imposing array of instruments; altimeters, fore-and-aft and lateral inclinometers, drift indicators—and five compasses. Five compasses—but not one of them could really be trusted for a heading, in this region so close to the earth's magnetic pole!

The two men would have to plot their course like the ancient Vikings, by taking "fixes" on the sun. (As it was summer, there would be no darkness in this part of the world, no visible stars.)

Here in the Arctic, where the earth's meridians converge, they faced a navigation problem far greater than that faced by Charles Lindbergh when he crossed the Atlantic the year before. Nor had the trans-Arctic flights of 1926 involved the same problem. Byrd, striking from Spitsbergen to the Pole and back, had paralleled a meridian. He had only to change direction once; at the Pole itself. The crew of the dirigible *Norge* had also followed a direct line, first north, in their case, and then south.

Eielson and Wilkins, wanting to explore new areas, planned to fly a curved path around the polar regions. This meant that they must cross meridians. They would have to change direction fifty times during the trip in order to maintain their course.

During part of the flight they would have to change direction every few minutes!

In the weeks before their departure on the history-making

journey Wilkins spent much time plotting the complicated navigation, using a special method and map prepared by the American Geographic Society.

This was to be a flight by and for science. Still, the two men knew, they must take a long gambling chance. Wilkins could not keep on course without taking fixes on the sun. Sight of the sun could mean the difference between success or failure, life or death. But what weather would they meet on their journey of more than 2,000 miles above this "blind spot of the globe?" There was no telling. As Barrow in that year had no radio station, they must set out without even a report on weather conditions at their distant destination.

In April, shortly before the departure, Eielson sat down in the old whaling station at the ice-locked town and wrote a letter to his brother Oliver.

Modern pilots would smile at his pride in the performance of his single-engine Vega. "We flew over here in 40 below weather making an average speed of 120 miles an hour," he wrote. "This plane certainly steps out when you give her the gas— makes 145 full out."

Imagine planning to cross the Arctic Ocean in a plane not much faster than an automobile!

"In a few days," he continued, in his usual terse and modest style, "we are going to cross the unexplored territory to the northeast. We hope to land at Kings Bay, Spitsbergen (2,200 miles away). . . . We have to take off with 3,500 pounds of gasoline, etc. If we smash on take-off, and there is always a good chance of it, I will not be able to get home till September —the first boat. The next mail does not leave here till August, but I am sending this letter with a fellow who leaves here to-morrow by dog team for Nome. . . . Best regards to all. . . .

Your brother

Ben

P.S. Expect to see you before you receive this letter."

A crowd of awe-struck Eskimos watched, on the morning of April 15, as Eielson and Wilkins climbed into their heavily loaded, brightly painted monoplane. The take-off was close. The Eskimos had cleared an ice runway between towering snowbanks, but the narrow, slick strip, scraped of all snow for utmost momentum, made Eielson's job a very exacting one.

Wilkins later wrote that he watched the tail planes swaying, missing one snow bank, then another by no more than a foot as the Vega gathered speed. "An error of a few pounds' pressure on the rudder, a swing of a few inches one way or the other, and . . . disaster would surely have followed. Eielson kept his nerve. . . . We lifted, swung sickeningly, touched the ice again—then soared smoothly into free air!"

The first eleven hours passed well. The weather was calm and clear. Wilkins worked constantly, checking the intricate course and taking notes on the unexplored ocean below. Now and then the men broadcast reports of their position, using a small, hand-driven generator. They had left a receiver with the Barrow school-teacher, asking him to listen for them. But they had no idea whether or not they would be heard.*

At midnight local time, flying at an altitude of 3,000 feet, they could still see the red orb of the sun. But trouble lay ahead.

---

* They were heard by the excited Barrow teacher. But the town's ice-locked isolation prevented him from telling the world about it for months.

Fog banks hung directly on their course. And "far, far away, in the very distant eastern sky, pillars of high storm clouds hung like wraiths under the pale, blue zenith."

Soon they were making their way through rolling mists. The clouds became thicker. The two men were in a sober mood. How bad was the weather ahead? They had left Barrow with barely enough gas to reach Spitsbergen and the gauge indicated that they had already used up more than expected. Wilkins checked the navigation with utmost care, knowing that there would be no fuel for any wasted flight.

They traveled a long time this way in silence, as clouds filled the sky. Then Eielson gave a shout and pointed out the window. The peaks of rugged mountains were in sight, rising majestic from the fog.

Wilkins smiled in triumph. This was Grant Land. They had come more than half way and were right on the course that he had set.

He opened a thermos of coffee and the two men celebrated with a breakfast of biscuits and pemmican. But the meal could not but be an uneasy one. The sky ahead, in the direction of Greenland, had been looking more and more threatening. By this time Wilkins was almost certain, from all signs of wind and temperature, that there must be a gale raging beyond at Spitsbergen.

"There are two courses open," he told Eielson. "Down there we can land. . . . Can we get off again? If we go on we will meet storm at Spitsbergen and perhaps never find the land. Do you wish to land now?"

Eielson hesitated, wriggled in his seat.

Then he replied, "I'm willing to go on and chance it."

Soon he was having to fight to fly. The temperature outside was 48 below zero, and the engine began to falter in the extreme cold. Time and again he was forced to advance the throttle full and climb steeply.

Cloud-banks now towered so high above the ice that it was impossible for the monoplane to top them. Eielson had to find a way between them, dodging right and left. Yet in all these maneuverings he managed to hold the course, skilfully making up for each deviation, Wilkins says, without his aid.

Toward the end of the long journey the Vega flew into violent winds and was "tossed like a cork on a stormy sea." It was all Eielson could do to keep the plane aloft. Wilkins was surprised by the fierceness of the storm in this season. He was later to learn that it was one of the worst gales that had struck the Spitsbergen region in the month of April in many years.

As the plane battled its way into a driving blizzard, the silence of the two pioneers now held a deep anxiety.

There was no turning back now.

There was almost no gas left in the tank.

In their fight for control in the angry gale, the task of keeping on course was becoming more and more difficult. Neither of the two men could help wondering, as they flew doggedly on, what the outcome would be.

Then, at last, they saw them: two needle-pointed peaks, looming up out of the murk. Land!

Eielson headed directly toward them, cutting altitude. It would be hard to imagine a more desperate airplane approach. Surface wind was furious. The windshield was so covered with blowing snow and salt spray that he could hardly see anything.

Suddenly a patch of smooth-looking, snow-covered land flashed by the windows—and a mountain loomed dead ahead!

Eielson missed the peak by a narrow margin. Swinging broadside to the wind and "crabbing" out to sea, he turned back again at once toward land. Again he had to swerve sharply to avoid mountains. "We were like an imprisoned bird," Wilkins has written, "beating against a window pane."

The windshield before Eielson was now so thick with snow and frozen oil that he had to rely on Wilkins, who had a better view out the side window to guide him: "Turn right . . . left . . . a bit more . . . turn back . . . Keep as close to the land as possible . . . THERE IT IS ON OUR RIGHT!"

Wilkins had managed to find the stretch of smooth-looking, snow-covered land which they had passed before.

Eielson circled short out to sea again and came back low. The men braced themselves as he leveled the Vega and lowered it steadily until it was lost in the swirling snow.

They felt the impact of the skis—and the Vega slowed to a rough but safe stop.

Once on the ground they could see no more than a few feet beyond the plane. Hurrying out into the blizzard, they inspected the Vega and found that it was not damaged. They drained the oil, stamped snow about the skis to keep them from freezing, tied protective covers over the engine. Then they climbed back into the plane and slept.

The storm continued for five days, as they waited, wondering exactly where they were. As soon as the weather broke they cleared the deep drifts from the plane and went to work laboriously tramping down a runway for take-off. It was a hard task for two men after such a storm. But after a few failures at take-off Eielson got the Vega into the air.

Almost at once, he and Wilkins sighted the tall radio masts and houses of Green Harbour, Spitsbergen.

A group of startled Scandinavians came skiing toward the trans-Arctic plane as it landed.

"Who are you?" they cried.

Eielson answered them in "Old Norse," the language of his grand-parents.

"This is Captain Wilkins," he said, quietly, with a modesty to equal that of Lindbergh's famous arrival speech in Paris. "We have come across from Alaska."

"Impossible!" the men shouted, laughing. "The plane is too small! And anyway you're speaking Norwegian."

But it was not long before wine was flowing freely at the Green Harbour radio station, and the message flashing out to an astonished world that Eielson and Wilkins, in a small, practically untried monoplane, had crossed the top of the world in twenty hours and twenty minutes.

"Arrived safely," Eielson wirelessed his father in North Dakota, who had had no news of him for many weeks. "Will be home soon."

It was in their newspapers that the Eielson family learned that the boy with the "flying craze" had become an international hero.

Returning through Europe, he and Wilkins were feted and honored by the rulers of Norway, Denmark, Sweden, Belgium, Holland, Germany, France and England. The Scandinavian government proudly awarded its Leiv Eiriksson Memorial

Medal to Eielson—"Transpolar Flyer of Norwegian Ancestry, for Viking Deed and Daring." In England, Wilkins was knighted by King George V.

"Never," declared Great Britain's Colonial Minister, "since Balboa stood on a peak in Darien and saw for the first time the broad Pacific, has so significant a new vision of the world been spread before human eyes in one day as when Wilkins flew . . . from America to Europe by way of the Arctic."

Back in the United States, the flyers received a big ovation in New York and proceeded west, amid great fanfare, to Eielson's home town. As he landed his famous Arctic plane on the hayfield where he had once landed his first Jenny, 5,000 North Dakotans, including the Governor, were waiting to greet him. Brass bands blared. Local pilots sporting helmets stood importantly among the crowd.

Eielson, wearing a summer suit and a straw hat, climbed smiling out of the cockpit into a swarm of eager reporters.

He seemed embarrassed by their questions. Quizzed about his Arctic hardships, he turned away.

"Twenty and a half hours and two meals," he said, "I guess that's all there was to it."

A neighbor who had known him since he was a boy asked him what his "greatest thrill" had been.

Gravely, he told her that it was when the French Air Minister's wife, "a charming girl," had asked him for a kiss.

Later, in a White House ceremony, President Herbert Hoover presented Eielson with the Harmon Trophy for the outstanding air contribution of 1928.

He was also awarded the Distinguished Flying Cross for "one of the most extraordinary accomplishments in all time."

Chapter 4: DEATH OF A GREAT AIRMAN

Eielson did not rest long on his laurels.

He joined Wilkins that very autumn in another exploring expedition, this time to the opposite end of the earth.

They were the first men to fly into the Antarctic. Striking south from Deception Island in the South Shetlands, shortly before Christmas, they covered a total air distance of 1,200 miles in the Far South regions and sighted six hitherto unknown islands.

This made them the first men in history to discover land from the sky.

Wilkins planned a second Antarctic expedition, in 1929, with Eielson at the controls. But their remarkable flying partnership was now broken. Eielson regretfully decided not to join him.

For the first time in his life, Eielson was giving thought to money. He was planning to be married, and he had earned less flying for the explorer than he would have earned at his old job teaching high school.

Beyond this, the Far North still drew him, with strong force. He had not forgotten his dream of thundering flight above Alaska and across the top of the world, and now that he was an international hero his words carried more weight than they had four years earlier.

In New York, he persuaded a large company, the Aviation Corporation, to put money into Alaska, merging some of the small, struggling air services that had sprung up there into a real airline. The Aviation Corporation agreed to furnish funds and larger planes, and agreed that if business proved promising enough it would later launch the first air service from the United States through Alaska to Asia.

The New York executives were not altogether convinced. Some of them thought Eielson's predictions visionary. But he told them that flight was bound to boom at the top of the world, and said he would prove it.

Now, to his family's surprise and his own, he was a well-paid airline executive. He was not to fly any more, under the terms of his contract. As Vice President and General Manager of the new Alaska company, he was to run the business from his desk, hiring other pilots to work for him in the air. But his family knew him too well to take comfort from this unlikely agreement. His brother Oliver, who was planning a trip to South America, threatened to cancel it unless he gave his word that he would stay on the ground.

"Otherwise," Oliver bluntly told him, "I'd just have to come home to bury you."

Ben finally promised.

"I guess," he said, smiling, almost as if he meant it, "it's time for me to settle down."

He returned to Fairbanks in the summer of 1929. His old friends at the log cabin town greeted him with a new respect and even some wariness. They wondered whether world fame and New York money might have turned his head. But they found him as friendly and modest in his well-tailored business suit, and as full of young enthusiasm, as he had once been in his fur parka.

"Now we'll really put Fairbanks on the map!" he told them.

He looked for important work for his airline, and soon found it. An American trading vessel, the motor ship *Nanuk,* was ice-bound that autumn off North Cape, Siberia, some 400 miles to the northwest of Alaska's Seward Peninsula. Fifteen passengers were trapped aboard her, and a load of fur. The *Nanuk's* owners offered Eielson $50,000 if his company would fly over and ferry the people and freight back to Alaska.

Eielson knew that it was a highly dangerous proposition; more dangerous, weather-wise, than the trans-Arctic flights he had made with Wilkins. The coastal region where America and Asia nearly touch at the top of the world, with only the 50-mile channel of Bering Strait between them, is one of brewing fogs and storms. Flying conditions along these shores are consistently worse than those out over the open spaces of the Arctic Ocean.

To the peril of bad weather would be added the handicap of Arctic winter darkness. His trans-Arctic flights with Wilkins had been made in summer. By the time he had made his terms with the *Nanuk's* owners, the month of October had set in. The northern parts of Alaska and Siberia would soon be shrouded in night during some twenty hours out of every twenty-four.

Despite these conditions, he decided that the flights must be made. This was the biggest transportation contract of any kind ever offered in the Far North. It would be a spectacular job. Success would give his New York employers full proof of what he had told them.

He signed the contract, and as promptly decided to break his promise to his brother. He did not want to sit at a desk, sending other men out on such dangerous journeys. The very thought was distasteful. He determined to make half of the trips to the *Nanuk* himself.

A game young Fairbanks mechanic named Earl Borland agreed to go with him, in an all-metal cabin Hamilton. One of the new airline's pilots, a pioneer named Frank Dorbandt, agreed to begin flights at the same time with a second mechanic, Bud Bassett, in a Stinson.

Young Borland was moody as the time for departure approached. He confided to friends that he had a strange feeling that he and Eielson would never return. Eielson, at a farewell supper, showed no sign of sharing his presentiment. He seemed full of confidence and high spirits. He "ate lots of ptarmigan and waffles," one of the guests remembers, "talked way past midnight about polar flying."

"We'll have a real party," Eielson gaily told the crowd, "as soon as we return."

Late in October the two planes were flown to Teller, a tiny coastal settlement not far from Bering Strait which was to serve as the jump-off point to Siberia.

Eielson and Dorbandt each made a successful first trip to the *Nanuk* and back, but the return journey was ominous. Blinded by blizzard, they were forced down and marooned for several days on the bleak Siberian coast. They made it back to Alaska during a brief clearing. Then another blizzard struck, and they were grounded at the Teller base for more than a week.

On the stormy morning of November 9, according to an eyewitness, Eielson and Dorbandt waited together in the Teller roadhouse. Eielson sat with his feet propped on a counter, reading a magazine. Dorbandt paced restlessly up and down the room.

Dorbandt was one of the ablest of the pioneers who had arrived in Alaska since Eielson's first flights, but he was a reckless and impulsive one. He was also hot-tempered and loud of mouth. Since Eielson's return to Alaska as airline manager, the two men had clashed more than once. Only a few weeks before, when Eielson had postponed a local flight because of bad weather, Dorbandt had accused his new boss of being a coward.

"When are we going to take off?" Dorbandt asked Eielson, on that fateful morning at Teller.

"We'll wait for the next weather report from the *Nanuk*," Eielson tersely told him.

Dorbandt tore a piece of wrapping paper from the roadhouse counter and scrawled a rough diagram of Bering Strait and the two continents.

"You know," he shouted, "all we have to do is hit right across here!"

Eielson did not reply.

"Well," Dorbandt told him, "you can sit there if you want. I'm leaving."

At 10:45 people in the roadhouse heard the roar of the Stinson's engine and saw Dorbandt's plane take off, heading toward Asia.

Eielson, without a word, walked upstairs and returned in his fur parka. His face was set as he and Borland went out to their plane. At 11:15 the Hamilton, too, bumped off the sea ice and disappeared into the gloomy sky to the west.

Some time later Dorbandt, foiled by dense fog in Bering Strait, returned.

Eielson and his mechanic did not return. Nor did they reach the *Nanuk.* Days passed. Weeks passed. There was only silence.

*

In all air history, no rescue expedition has been tried in the face of greater and more disheartening obstacles than the search for Ben Eielson.

Soon after he disappeared, the sun dropped below the horizon, not to rise until the spring of the following year. Only a few dim hours around noon, each day, were light enough for flying.

The temperature dropped to forty below zero. Repeated gales with winds of near-hurricane force began to sweep between the two continents. The weather that winter was to be far stormier than usual. The manager of the Teller roadhouse, an old-timer in this region, later said that he had never seen so much ice, snow, wind and fog.

When Alaska's other pioneer pilots learned that Eielson was missing they decided—almost to a man—to fly over to Siberia and search for him.

They had a hard time even reaching Teller. Joe Crosson, a

rugged young pilot from California who was Eielson's close friend, arrived first at the gale-lashed jump-off point. Others were blocked by storm and accidents. It was not until December that the small group of flyers and mechanics gathered at Teller, ready for take-off to Asia, and the weather was still so violent that Crosson had not yet been able to cross Bering Strait a single time.

Crowded together in the frame roadhouse, the men looked out past high snowbanks each morning to dense fog or whirling blizzard. Day after day, the foul weather continued. Weather at the *Nanuk* was reported by the ship's wireless as no better. "Ceiling and visibility nil nil," the vessel flashed, over and over. "High winds."

The expedition's small planes represented all the flyable craft in Alaska at the time. Anchored on the ice against the wind, they were a pitiful sight. Modern pilots to whom the ships are described find it hard to believe that Arctic winter flights to Asia were even considered in such aircraft, quite apart from the storm. None of the planes had range enough to fly non-stop from Teller to the *Nanuk*. None had any but the crudest of instruments. All but one, a small Stinson biplane, were open-cockpit!

For comfort and safety, none of them could compare with the all-metal cabin Hamilton in which Eielson and his mechanic had disappeared.

With each day of inaction the grounded pilots became more anxious and restless. Dorbandt was reported to be verging on a nervous breakdown. Eielson's friends knew that he and Borland had carried emergency provisions to last thirty days. As the days passed, desperate tries were made to cross to Siberia in spite of the weather. Time and again a pilot took off from the frozen sea, only to return. Even these hops were hazardous. Dorbandt, landing on the rough ice before the roadhouse, broke an axle on one try, a ski on another and a landing gear on the third.

An appeal for help was made to the Army Air Corps in Washington. The reply was flat; the Army was unable to assist. It had no properly equipped planes, no men experienced in Arctic winter flying. Had another pilot been lost so far north in winter, Washington would have known of only one flyer well qualified to go to his rescue: Ben Eielson.

More cheering news came from other quarters. In New York Explorer Stefansson had suggested that the government appeal for help to the Soviet Union, which was known to have done considerable pioneer air work in the Arctic. The State Department could not make the appeal; Washington, in that year, had not yet recognized the Soviet government. But the Secretary of the Interior and the Chairman of the Senate Foreign Relations committee had sent telegrams, and the Russians had replied promptly. Moscow was sending Siberians with dog teams to the region where Eielson might have crashed. It was offering a reward amounting to a thousand dollars for news of the lost plane. It had also ordered Soviet planes to fly to northeast Siberia for search work.

Eielson's New York employers were also taking steps for his rescue. The Aviation Corporation had hired a group of Canadian pilots and mechanics to join the Alaskan pilots at Teller, with three ski-equipped cabin Fairchilds. There would be some delay, however. The company felt that it would be too dangerous for the Canadian planes to fly north to Alaska at this time of year. They were to be crated and shipped by boat from Seattle, as soon as they could be assembled.

For Joe Crosson this was not soon enough. By this time forty days had passed since Eielson and Borland had disappeared. On the stormy morning of December 17 Crosson loaded his plane, a small Waco, with extra fuel and provisions to last several weeks.

A young pilot named Harold Gillam also prepared to leave, in a Stearman. The others were astonished by his nerve. Gillam was not an experienced flyer. He had just soloed, and had made only one cross-country trip. But he did not seem to know the meaning of caution. "Give me a ship!" he had begged Eielson's assistants at the airline office. "Give me a ship! I want to look for Ben." They had hesitated, but in the end he had had his way, and he was just as determined to leave with Crosson now.

It was a gloomy little crowd that watched as Crosson and Gillam, bundled heavily in furs, climbed into their open-cockpit ships for take-off. Since they had no radio contact with each other, it was agreed that Gillam would follow his more experienced friend closely and come down to land if Crosson did. The small engines roared, the pilots waved and the planes disappeared into the angry sky. The others expected that they would return, as they had so often before, but this time they made it.

The flight across to Asia was harrowing, as Crosson later described it. Heavy fog "boiled up" from the broken ice, he said, and winds funneling through Bering Strait "seemed to blow in twenty-three directions at once." He and Gillam flew low, fighting for control. Visibility was "close to zero." Heading stubbornly northwest, they navigated "half-blind," keeping contact by following the black streaks made by leads of open water below.

They had been in the air for nearly two hours when they sighted a low, snow-covered bluff: the shore of Siberia.

The fog was thinner here, but darkness was almost upon them. Crosson began to follow the winding, white, treeless bank around, hoping to find some sign of a village before nightfall. He was rewarded at length by the sight of a cluster of huts in the white, and brought his Waco down on the ice close by. Gillam landed in his tracks.

A group of Soviet Eskimos came trudging through the snow to meet the planes. They were dressed in strange skin clothing, Crosson said; "separate hoods like helmets, we'd never seen them in Alaska. And they had fur mittens made of the foreheads of reindeer." Surprisingly matter-of-fact, the Russians helped Crosson and Gillam drain the oil, cover the motors and pull the sleeping bags from their planes. They then led them to an oval-shaped hut, where they were greeted by a broad-smiling Eskimo named "Kacherb" who was the village Chief.

It was a tense moment for the two Americans as they drew a rough sketch of the two continents and a cabin plane headed northwest. Had the Chief any news of Eielson's Hamilton?

The Eskimo nodded, his eyes full of excitement.

He told Crosson, by means of sketches, gestures and strange guttural words, that he knew about the strange plane. His people had seen it fly overhead, that many weeks ago. He took the pencil and sketched the direction in which it had been heading: toward the *Nanuk*.

Late the next morning, when the dimness of brief day returned, Crosson and Gillam refueled their planes from the extra gas carried in the cabins and took off once more into a threatening sky.

It was not long before they flew into a blizzard. Crosson decided to turn back. He rocked the wings as a signal for Gillam to follow. Then "everything blotted out." He lost sight of Gillam's plane and of the earth as well.

He flew blind for a few anxious minutes, till he caught sight of a pressure ridge in the ocean below, found the dim line of the shore again, and followed it back to the village. His goggles froze over as he approached for landing. He was forced to push them back, and as a result "frosted" his eyes. This ailment was to add much to his trials in the weeks to come.

Gillam did not return that evening. Crosson spent a sleepless night worrying about him. The next day, striking out again to the westward, he scanned the snowy shores, hunting for two lost comrades instead of one. He flew three hours alone in the dimness, without seeing anything on the bleak, wintry earth below.

Then he sighted a welcome scatter of specks in the white; "like pepper," he later said, "spilled on a table-cloth." As he came down he saw that some made a thin line along the shore: the trading village of North Cape. Two specks lay out on the ice: the *Nanuk* and a Soviet ship, also ice-locked: the *Stavropol*. There was a fourth speck on the ice nearby. As Crosson landed he saw with astonishment that it was Gillam's Stearman. The nervy little fellow had somehow battled his way alone through the blizzard and reached the *Nanuk* the night before!

Lodging aboard the motor ship, Crosson and Gillam prepared to begin at last the long-delayed search for Eielson. Once more they were blocked from action. The most ferocious storm of the whole winter struck on the day after their arrival at the *Nanuk* and continued for more than a month. Snow and wind. Wind and snow. Thick, rolling fog. Men traveling by dog team lost their way in this blizzard. On only eight days out of a five-week period was it even remotely possible for a plane to fly.

"It is the tradition of exploration," the great Stefansson has written, "not to give up rescue work so long as there is any reasonable chance." Never has this tradition been more gallantly honored than by the two young Alaskans in their open-cockpit planes. The chance would no longer be called very reasonable, but they risked their own lives anyway.

On the eight mornings when the storm seemed to be abating they hurried out into the darkness and dug their planes, sheltered in snow-block hangars, from the deep drifts. They laboriously warmed the engines, heated the oil, and took off as soon as it was light enough to fly. One heading north, the other south, they scouted the coastline and struck as far inland as they could.

The weather was still bad, even on these days. There were frequent snow flurries, and in the rolling gloom, Crosson said, it was always very difficult to tell the snow-covered earth from the heavy sky.

"It was like flying inside a milk bottle," he reported.

They searched most often near the mouth of the Amguyema River, some sixty miles east of the *Nanuk,* where a Siberian trapper had reported to Soviet authorities that he had seen a strange plane. Both Crosson and Gillam returned to this region several times. Each told the other that he had a strong hunch, as he cruised above the area, that Eielson's ship was down not far away. But neither found any sign there, or anywhere else, of the Hamilton.

Back in Alaska, the rest of the pilots were still storm-bound. The Canadian planes, arrived at last by steamer at a southeast port, had had more than one accident as their pilots tried to fly them north to Teller. They finally reached the jump-off point in mid-January. Spirits improved on both sides of the Strait, and hope increased with the news that Soviet planes were also approaching the *Nanuk*.

The search for America's lost pioneer was now featured in headlines throughout the world.

"A big aerial drive is under way," the Associated Press flashed from Nome. "Airplanes manned by American, Russian and Canadian aviators are today either moving toward North Cape, Siberia, or poised at various places in Alaska and Siberia awaiting favorable weather for massed attack to solve the mystery of (Eielson's) fate."

"The combined Soviet Union, Canadian and American groups," the New York *Times* reported, "represent the greatest rescue armada ever assembled in the Arctic."

Continued storm, however, prevented this great armada from reaching northeast Siberia in time to join the search.

Not until January 25 was there a change in the weather.

That morning Crosson and Gillam stood in front of the *Nanuk* and watched a heartening sight: the sun, rising red and low on the horizon, returned to the Arctic for another year.

The sky was clear at last.

The two flyers, who had nearly exhausted the local stock of fuel, decided to make a trip back to Alaska for a fresh supply.

"We'll be back," they told the people aboard the *Nanuk*.

They took off together toward the east.

Those aboard the motor ship were surprised, just a few hours later, to hear the roar of engines in the sky and recognize the two planes returning. A crowd hurried toward them as they taxied to a stop.

Crosson climbed out of the cockpit, his face drawn.

"Well," he said slowly, "the search is over."

He reached back into his Waco and pulled out a mass of crumpled metal.

"From Ben's plane," he said, and turned, walking abruptly toward the *Nanuk* to hide his feelings.

Supper aboard the ship that night was an awkward meal. Crosson and Gillam were hardly able to tell their story. They had been flying low and close together, scouting the coast along the way. As they'd neared the Amguyema River trapper's hut they had seen something that they had not seen in the gloom of winter. They had noticed what seemed to be a dark streak on the sunlit snow.

Crosson had thought at first that it was a dog team. But he wasn't sure; "It seemed to lay at a peculiar angle." He'd dropped down for a closer look, and Gillam, too, had cut altitude.

Not until they were as low as 300 feet had they seen that the dark streak was a shadow cast by the wing of an airplane sticking up out of the snow.

They'd landed and run through the deep drifts to the wreck of Eielson's Hamilton.

The aircraft lay on a mound, pointing southeast toward Alaska. One side of the fuselage was shorn away and the tail was torn off just aft of the cabin.

Digging into the cockpit, they'd found the walls crushed, the seats mashed, the safety belts hanging empty. There had been no sign of Eielson or Borland. They must have been hurled from the wreckage, probably to instant death.

By all signs, the crash had been violent and uncontrolled.

How had it happened? Eielson must have been circling the trapper's hut, planning to land for the night. As he banked the plane, a wing must have struck the snowy mound. He must have misjudged his altitude in the confusing white of winter earth and sky, all the more confusing because it was dusk. The trapper had reported that it was twilight when he saw the strange plane fly over and the stopped hands of the Hamilton's clock confirmed this.

No one would ever be sure, but this was Crosson's and Gillam's guess as to how the great airman had met his death.

The day after discovery of the wreck Soviet, Canadian and Alaskan planes, also freed by the return of good weather, arrived at the *Nanuk*. They joined in the job of hauling men and supplies to the scene of disaster, and a group of Siberian Eskimos began the grim task of digging for the dead. Camping in tents beneath the Hamilton's wing, the Russians labored for weeks in the sub-zero weather, hacking trenches through sub-surface snow that was packed almost as hard as cement.

On February 5 the Hamilton's motor base, stained with blood, was found fifty feet from the plane. The next day a pair of pilot's glasses was uncovered. On February 9, scattered airplane parts: ailerons, ventilators and other sections. Three days later, Borland's mittens. The next day Borland's body was found.

It was not until February 18, three weeks after discovery of the wreck, that the body of Eielson was uncovered, deep in the snow a hundred and twenty feet from the plane.

"It was a great relief that this wearisome and nerve-straining search was concluded," one of the Russians wrote in his diary, "but it was a mournful day for us all."

A Soviet pilot named Maurice Slepnev flew the bodies of Eielson and Borland to the steamer *Stavropol,* and a doctor on board prepared the bodies for burial. They were then wrapped in American flags. Crosson and the other Americans were surprised and touched by this honoring gesture. They had not thought that it would be possible, as they had no flags with them. But Siberian Eskimo women at nearby North Cape fashioned some home-made ones of red and blue muslin and white ship's canvas, with every star in place.

"Those Russians did everything in their power for us," Crosson later said, "and they wouldn't take a cent in pay. They were swell people." One of his proudest possessions for the rest of his life was a Soviet air medal later given to him, Gillam and a third Alaska pilot, Ed Young, by Pilot Slepnev. They, in a gesture of appreciation for Slepnev's help, had given him a gun. Very moved, he had told them, "I will make you a gift of the most precious thing I own." The shining red medal, which he had been awarded by his government for Arctic accomplishment, showed an airplane silhouetted against a snowy peak. Slepnev had had a message engraved on the back: ED JOE AND HAROLD—MY BROTHERS AND FRIENDS.

Late in February, on the wind-swept ice before the *Nanuk* and the *Stavropol,* America formally took custody of her own.

Both vessels' flags hung at half-mast on that foggy morning. The chairman of the Chukotsk region of Siberia, who had traveled more than 400 miles by dog team to be present at the ceremony, spoke his sorrow that the tragic loss had happened on Soviet soil. An American pilot expressed our thanks for Russian aid. The bodies were drawn slowly by sled to a Canadian cabin plane that was to carry them home, lifted inside, and the windows were shrouded with black.

Storm delayed the sad journey, as it had delayed the search. Two weeks passed before the plane was able to leave for Alaska. It was escorted, with special permission from Washington and Moscow, by an honoring Soviet plane with Slepnev at the controls.

Violent weather and solemn pomp attended the body of the young pilot all the way on its long, slow journey back to North Dakota. Rough wind and water tossed the steamer on her voyage south from Alaska to Seattle. Crowds thronged the water front when she docked, and the city observed a moment of silence. Thousands later filed past the coffin, which was draped with American and Soviet flags. Army caissons rumbled and planes circled overhead as it was taken to the railroad station in a driving rainstorm.

The locomotive that drew Eielson's funeral train across the western states was draped with black. Many thousands stood at stations along the way to watch it pass. Thousands more stood bareheaded in the Hatton graveyard, in a sudden blizzard, as the coffin was lowered into the family plot.

Proposals had been made that Eielson be buried with full military honors at Arlington. His father had decided against this. "So many people are buried there," he told reporters. "After all, what is fame?"

Today a large modern air base, not far from the site of the Fairbanks ball park, has been named in honor of Eielson.

History has paid him the best tribute, a living one.

Today Alaskans who once scanned the sky anxiously for the speck of his flimsy De Havilland seldom look up as a never-ending procession of planes thunders overhead; small planes striking out over the wilderness, large planes striking out over the polar sea or to Asia.

The earnest young flyer had been sure that it would come. It was as certain as the power of his Liberty engine to lift him over a mountain. He had figured on it and, in the way of the pioneer, cheerfully had worked for it till the end.

Chapter 5: NOEL WIEN

The Cautious Dean

Noel Wien is one of the few early pioneers who have escaped
death in flight. Today he is considered the dean of Alaskan
aviation. Arriving in the Far North from Minnesota in 1924,
two years after Eielson, he went to work and logged a total of
10,000 hours above mountains, tundra and sea. He still flies
occasionally.

Wien also brought three of his brothers to Alaska. First it was
Ralph, who soloed in 1928 and flew with remarkable courage
until he was killed in an Arctic crash. Then it was Fritz, who
became one of the ablest mechanics at the Fairbanks field. Sig
followed much later and pioneered the first regular air service
to the farthest-north town of Barrow, in the nineteen forties.

With time these Minnesota farm boys of Scandinavian descent became leading citizens of our last frontier. There is no
family more respected in Alaska today than the Wien family.

Everybody looks up to them. Not even the Governor of the Territory enjoys such wide prestige.

Meeting Noel Wien is a surprise. He is a tall, conservative-looking man, baldish, with a ring of graying hair, a tight-drawn mouth and a close-clipped, soft way of speaking. He is obliging, patient, known for his unusual kindliness toward other people. Except for a sort of weathered look, he might be taken for a small-town preacher.

Wien is a Mason and a Presbyterian. He does not drink. He does not smoke. Unlike most of Alaska's bush pilots, he does not swear, nor does he drive an automobile like a race-car. He navigates his car slowly and carefully through the Fairbanks streets. He and his family live in a large white frame house with pale yellow shutters, near the airfield. As you sit with him in the comfortable living room, bright with flowered chintz and full book-shelves, only paintings of snowcaps on the walls suggest that you're in Alaska, and it is hard to believe that this gentle man was one of the first air pioneers.

He is modest, as he tells about his flying, frugal with words. "A good trip," he'll say, of a long, lone journey above un-mapped wilds. "Poor weather," he'll say, of a howling blizzard. He speaks of a historic air journey as if it were a small bicycle excursion.

But when he talks of the early days, his eyes keen with mem-ory, people listen spell-bound, for the story is not a gentle one, and he is one of the few men left to tell it.

Noel Wien and his brothers grew up on a homestead near Cook, Minnesota. Their father was a grain farmer. As a boy, Noel was bored by farming. His interest in aviation began very early, before he had ever seen a plane. He borrowed every book on flying that he could get his hands on and told his sceptical family he wanted to be a pilot. He went to work for the county road system, when he was older, and saved enough money to take lessons. Then, against his father's wishes, he left home and went to the Twin Cities, where there was a flying school. He was 22, by this time, and had seen planes, but only from a distance, as they clattered high above the family grain fields.

After eight hours of dual instruction, at forty dollars an hour, he was ready to solo, but he did not have enough money to do so. Flying was considered so risky, he discovered, that the school wouldn't let him take up a plane alone unless he made a deposit of $2,800 to cover the price of the ship.

Discouraged, he hung around the dusty airfield, enviously watching pilots who were rich enough to raise this sum or to own their own planes. He wheedled them to take him up.

One day a barnstormer agreed to take him along for a ride in a dual-control ship. The fellow had a lot of trouble trying to land on a short corn field. Wien's fingers itched as he watched him make two passes, overshooting each time. Suddenly the young farm boy's impatience was too much. Impulsively, he opened the throttle, took the plane around, and brought it down to a neat landing himself.

It was this that gave him his start. The barnstormer was so surprised by his skill and decision that he let him take the plane up alone and carry half the passengers. The job ended, however, when the barnstormer left the State.

In those days Wien was a lanky, blond boy who would do almost anything to make a living in the air instead of going back to the farm. It wasn't easy. "Pilots weren't considered much," he says, with one of his faint smiles. "People thought you might be all right or you might be crazy. They'd put up big picture posters of you at county fairs, but nobody would give you a steady job."

He worked a while for a large stunt circus called Federated Flyers. "I'd loop with the wing-walkers," he says. "People would scream and faint. The only trouble was that I had to ride a motorcycle and play auto polo part of the time." When the circus season ended, he signed for still more troublesome work.

A man named Hinck arrived in Minnesota, looking for a pilot to work in Mexico. There was a small revolution on down there, Hinck said. He was the agent for one of the factions, and he wanted a man to go to Veracruz, fly out over the enemy, and drop home-made dynamite bombs. Wien didn't like the sound of the job, but it seemed to be the only way to stay a pilot, so he took it. Hinck paid his fare to New Orleans and told him to wait there for further instructions.

He waited and waited. No instructions came, and no money. The plane that he was to fly, shipped collect, sat in a crate in the railroad station; he did not have the funds to claim it. He spent an angry two months at New Orleans, living much of the time on bananas. Then he read in a newspaper that the Mexican uprising was all over. There was nothing to do but go home.

It was not long after this disappointing adventure that another man turned up in Minnesota looking for a pilot. He was a stocky, energetic little fellow from Fairbanks, Alaska, named Jimmy Rodebaugh. He told Wien he had worked a while as a conductor on Alaska's railroad, also made a lot of money trading in furs. Now, he said, he was going to start a flying company.

Rodebaugh talked excitedly of Ben Eielson's pioneer flights out of Fairbanks the year before. He said that Alaskans were "crazy for aviation." He had come to the States to buy two planes, he told Wien, and to hire men to fly them. He seemed disappointed when Wien told him that he had only 500 hours in the air. He wanted an "experienced pilot," he said. But he offered to pay his fare north and a salary of $300 a month, guaranteed, if he would go to work for him.

Wien didn't know whether or not to believe his story. He was afraid the whole thing would end like the Mexican fiasco. Still, Rodebaugh seemed honest and full of real enthusiasm. Maybe there was work for pilots on a frontier. Deciding to take the chance, he traveled west and boarded a steamer from Seattle to Alaska. After all, one of Rodebaugh's planes was in the hold, and it wasn't shipped collect!

He got off the boat at the southeast port of Seward and took the rough railroad train, as Eielson had before him. But he didn't go straight to his Fairbanks base. He stopped at a large town called Anchorage where Rodebaugh had told him to spend a few weeks stunting and taking customers up for joyrides.

The dusty stretch which he had to use for a runway at Anchorage was the oddest one he'd ever seen; there was a road running right through it! "But the autos were really no trouble at all," he remembers. "There was only my plane, at the time, and people were on the lookout for me." His plane was not much, either; just a little war trainer, a Standard. At least Rodebaugh had replaced its small engine with a more powerful

Hispano-Suiza, and he'd had a tinner install an extra gas tank in the center section for more range.

Wien found that his eager little employer had told no lies. People in this north country really were "crazy for aviation." Ben Eielson's work had stirred their imaginations, and they'd crowd around the Standard clamoring for a chance to go up. They'd pay ten dollars apiece for hops, twice as much as people were willing to pay in Minnesota. A pilot was respected up here. The Anchorage newspaper even ran a big story about Wien, solemnly quoting what he had told reporters at the field: "Air conditions in Alaska are apparently the same as in the States."

He had not been long at Anchorage when he got orders to make his first long cross-country trip in the Far North. Rodebaugh sent him a message to fly the Standard on to its Fairbanks base, 300 miles away.

It would be the first plane trip ever made between the two towns. No airfields of any kind lay between them, and the Standard, even with its extra gas tank, would have barely enough range for a one-way journey. But Wien didn't expect any trouble. Anchorage and Fairbanks were connected by rail, and he could navigate by following the track all the way. Darkness would be no threat, this time of year. It was June, and the sun was up all around the clock.

To be extra sure of the weather, Wien sent telegrams to station agents at little rail stops en route, asking them to "step out and take a look at the sky." On the warm, clear evening of July 6, good reports clicked back; clear all the way, and he and a mechanic named William Yunker took off.

For two hours Wien followed the steel over the land without

any difficulty. His plane soared high in night sunshine among giant snowcaps, till the twisting track in the canyon below was only a thread of silver. Then the peaks sank behind, and the railroad led out across the rolling, mottled tundra. Flying in Alaska seemed easy enough, he thought, and he had never seen such magnificent country.

Trouble lay ahead, however; trouble of the most unlikely kind.

What was that thick, white stuff, rolling and swirling in the valley beyond? Fog? On these inland flats, on this crystal-clear summer night?

Wien and his mechanic exchanged puzzled glances. As they drew closer, they could hardly believe their eyes—and their noses. It wasn't fog, but smoke! There was a fire ahead!

Flames, doubtless started by a locomotive spark, were sweeping wildly across the tundra. It was one of the vast, uncontrolled wilderness fires that ravage parts of Alaska even to this day. Wien was more and more anxious as the track led him straight toward the conflagration. How long would he be able to keep sight of the railroad? The billowing smoke rolled up so thick, as he flew on, that soon he could see no more than a quarter of a mile—fifteen seconds' flying time—ahead of the plane.

He couldn't turn back; he hadn't enough fuel left to return to Anchorage. Nor, tempting as it was, did he dare to leave the railroad. He'd heard too many stories about how Eielson had lost his way in this country.

He was trapped. Lower and lower, he was forced, until he was speeding just over the winding rails. Dark slopes were flashing past, just beyond the wing tips. Suppose he should meet a train?

"It was rather scary," he says, quietly.

It was even more dangerous than he realized. He flew out of the smoke at last, close to Fairbanks, and landed safely at the town ball park. Shaking hands with Rodebaugh, he told his new employer about the smoky journey.

"I just hugged the track," he explained.

Rodebaugh looked horrified. "But what did you do?" he asked, "when you came to the sixty-foot overhead bridge at Dead Man's Slough?"

Wien paled. "Bridge? Was there a bridge?"

He thinks he must have flown under it.

He and a second pilot named Arthur Sampson flew busily that summer, speeding miners back into the hills, hauling meat, machinery, Malamute dogs and gold dust. This was solid work. The miners were willing to pay a dollar a mile to travel by air. There were more passengers than the planes could handle. One day Wien collected a total of $1,500 for Rodebaugh's company. By fall, two thirds of the cost of the Standards had been earned.

Rodebaugh looked forward to as busy a winter. But Wien disappointed him. When the first snow fell, and the temperature dropped steeply, he angered his employer by announcing that he would not make any cross-country trips till the following spring. The planes were too small, he said. He didn't like what he had heard about Fairbanks' sub-Arctic winters. Forced landings in the wilds would be too dangerous.

Wien's flying record in the Far North is something of a contradiction. He had none of Eielson's restless earnestness, none of the devil-may-care rashness of other early pilots. Not only did he refuse to fly in winter, the first year he arrived. He shunned storms, Rodebaugh complained, as he shunned whiskey. Today, among Alaska's younger pilots, Wien has the reputation of always having been very conservative. "Take 'em out and bring 'em back," they say. "Never been much fireworks to Noel."

They are right, in a sense, but they underestimate him. They forget that when he arrived in Alaska all cross-country trips were bold ones. They forget that Wien once disappeared into the Arctic, in a plane without radio or navigational aids, and was missing for three weeks. To "take 'em out and bring 'em back," in those days, was no mean feat. Wien made dozens of flights over hills that had never echoed to the roar of an engine. He made countless landings on rough terrain that had never known human foot-prints. Suspiciously but steadily, he pioneered.

The truth is that he is a pilot who repeatedly accomplished daring work in a cautious way.

Almost every landing was an experiment. Once, soon after his arrival in the north, he flew some passengers on his first trip into the rugged country surrounding Mt. McKinley. "I was able," he says, quite off-hand, as if it were nothing at all, "to land them within sixteen miles of where they wanted to go. The sand bar was 300 feet long, with uneven gravel at one end. This made me put first one wing on the gravel, then the other, as I came down. I tore off a little of the trailing edge of the wing. But it saved me from running into a log and some bushes."

Such risks were routine, and when Wien heard that a miner named Charles Opdyke was critically ill, without a doctor, out at a remote camp called Nome Creek, he took more than a routine chance to save him. Arriving over the sick man's cabin, Wien circled a while, studying the deep-ridged, wooded terrain. He saw only one place where landing might be possible: a hilltop.

The space was short. The angle was sharp. The hill was strewn with boulders. It was the only possible runway.

As he landed, his plane met the earth with a sickening jar. Three inches were broken off the wooden propeller. He had come prepared for such an emergency, with an extra prop lashed to the fuselage. He hastily installed it and loaded the sick man aboard.

Then he took off down the rocky hillside. As the plane roared down the slope the tops of spruce trees rose up just ahead and there was a moment when he didn't think he was going to make it. The Standard barely got up enough momentum to miss the branches as it lumbered into the air, heading back toward town.

Compared to the old logbooks of most pilots, Wien's logbook of his early flying in Alaska is surprisingly vivid. From the first, the frontier work seems to have intrigued him, and many lively details are inscribed in his neat hand.

There were good days:

"Made trip to Livengood, OK 1st one"
"Beef, meat, freight Brooks"
"Brooks, 1 passenger over, $1,000 gold dust back"

There were bad days:

"Joe Meherin, salesman passenger, nosed over in mud"

"Low ceiling, landed on small sand bar"

"Caribou Creek, 1 passgr over, made landing, nosed over, broke prop"

"Fairbanks-Brooks, 400 lb. beef, air release came out, hand pump saved day"

He also found time, like most of Alaska's bush pilots, to enjoy a little sport in the wild country.

"Dove on caribou Wickersham dome"

"Circle Springs—passenger back. Shot at bear"

Wien, not Eielson, was the first pilot in Alaska to fly across the Arctic Circle and make a landing on the north side. He made this flight in 1925, the year Eielson spent in the United States after the cancellation of his mail contract. The passengers on Wien's historic hop were two mining operators who wanted to travel from Fairbanks, 120 miles south of the Circle, to Wiseman, a mountain-cradled Arctic town 80 miles above it.

Miners at Wiseman, celebrating the first arrival of a plane at their settlement, initiated Wien into Alaska's most distinguished brotherhood, the honorary order of Pioneers.

On his return flight to Fairbanks he had a rougher initiation into the ranks of the trail-blazers.

He flew into sudden wind, over the Rampart Hills. The violent gusts swept his small plane sideways, far off course. Darkness fell. The gas in the tank ran out. He was forced to land on a sand bar in the wilds. He had not come prepared for such an accident. He had only a couple of dried buns in the plane, for food.

The next morning he started walking, following a compass

course in the direction which he hoped would lead him to a town. The going was far worse than he expected; spring break-up time had come to the north, and the earth was a soggy swamp. He waded through slush, stumbled over "niggerheads," bent trees, fighting his way through a kind of a jungle. Perhaps, he reflected, winter forced landings would be better, after all.

He drank snow for water, but got thirstier and thirstier. Hungrier and hungrier, he managed to shoot a few rabbits, and roasted them over camp-fires.

Three rivers lay across his path. One was still frozen solid enough to cross carefully on foot. The other two were swollen torrents. He was forced to build small rafts, wrapped around with willow-boughs, and float across. It took him three hard-fought days to travel the forty miles between his plane and the nearest town.

Wien had been less than a year in Alaska when Rodebaugh sent him back to the United States to buy a large plane. Aviation was booming so, despite frequent accidents, that a new, more important flying company was formed. All up and down the main street of Fairbanks merchants and miners dug into their pockets. More pilots were hired, and the town decided that it must have a real airliner, a regular cabin plane.

Wien had trouble finding one. Alaska, it seemed, was ahead of the nation. No cabin planes were for sale, in 1925, in the United States. There was a Waco model, he wired his employers, but he didn't trust it; it had not yet been tested for stress. There was a Bellanca being built which looked like a good ship, but it wouldn't be ready for six months.

That was too long, his employers wired back. Fairbanks couldn't wait.

Finally, at Curtiss Field, Long Island, he found a second-hand Fokker that had been built in Holland. It was just what the town wanted; large and spacious, fifty-four foot wingspread, 156 cubic feet in the cabin, fancy upholstery like a car, heavy 180 horsepower. German engine. It cruised at 90 miles an hour. The only trouble, he warned his employers, was that the plane was really rather large and fast-landing for a country without airfields.

His employers refused to be discouraged by this technical matter. They sent Wien $9,500 to buy the Fokker, and another $400 to have it shipped to Alaska by boat via the Panama Canal.

"At last," the Fairbanks *News-Miner,* proudly announced, "the Friendly North has passed from the Dog Team Stage into the Airship Class!"

As Wien had warned that it would be, the Fokker was a disappointment when it arrived in Alaska. Most of the pilots at Fairbanks refused to fly it. They called it a "haywire foreign rig." They said that its cockpit arrangement was dangerous, that it landed much too fast. How could a plane like that come down on a river bar? Even the new Fairbanks field, which had been smoothed from a vacant lot outside town, was too short.

Wien was the only pilot who would ever take the Dutch plane off the ground. The others were surprised that he dared. He did not fly it much; only 140 hours, in all. Even at Fairbanks, he says, he had to "pull it into a near stall at treetop level and then give it a little drop for three-point landing." But the fact remains that he flew it, and he seems to have had a curious fondness for the odd craft. He says he liked the reliable, six-cylinder engine—"so heavily built, no trouble at all." He still keeps the propeller as a souvenir.

It was in the Fokker that Wien made another historic trip; the first commercial flight from Fairbanks to Nome, 540 miles to the west at the edge of the Bering Sea. Only the Black Wolf Squadron, the Army flyers who had hedge-hopped from the States to Alaska and back in 1920, had flown the route before.

Wien's flight blazed a trail in mining as well as aviation history. His passenger, an engineer named Norman Stines, was making surveys for the United States Smelting, Refining and Mining Company of Boston. As a result of Stines' reports, great mechanical dredges were to be built outside Fairbanks and Nome, revolutionizing mining methods and bringing a new boom to the gold industry.

In June of 1925 Stines offered to pay $1,000 for the flight to Nome. The time saving would be well worth the price. No railroad led to the town, no road, and it would have taken him as long as six weeks to make the trip by roundabout river and ocean transport.

Wien had not yet made so long a flight in Alaska, but his employers assured him that it should be easy. He had only to follow the Tanana and Yukon rivers, they said, and there were "lots and lots of flat sand bars—dandy places to land." Also, there was a telegraph station about half way, at the town of Ruby, and it would flash a report to Fairbanks as the Fokker passed.

It was seven in the evening when Wien, with his brother Ralph riding as mechanic, took off toward Nome, heading into a bright sky. He preferred to fly at night in summer-time, he says; the air was usually smoother than during the day. As the plane roared westward Stines and two women secretaries were in good spirits, playing a game of cards back in the cabin, stopping now and then to admire the snowy splendor of Mt. McKinley.

Up front the Wien brothers were not in good spirits. Peering down at the Yukon River, they saw that all the "dandy sand bars" were submerged. The river was running high. There would be no safe landing place for this big plane, in case of emergency, all the way to Nome.

They flew on and passed the log cabin town of Ruby on schedule. Soon after this drops of rain began sliding down the panes. The Fokker entered the edge of a rain squall. It was not a bad storm, but Wien decided to turn back. As the plane no longer had enough fuel to return to Fairbanks, he decided to land at Ruby. If worse came to worst, crack-up beside a settlement would be better than crack-up in the wilds.

The passengers forgot their card game as he made several low passes above the village. Stines later said that he could hardly believe his eyes. Was that fool pilot really going to try to land here? The only possible runway was a short hillside which sloped up at a thirty degree angle, levelling out onto a small baseball diamond. It looked like suicide.

As slowly as possible, Wien eased the $9,500 airliner onto the upslope. Hurtling over the hilltop, the Fokker ran part way down the other side. Then the wheels broke through a patch of soft ground. The big plane nosed up and rocked clumsily over on its back. The propeller was split in two.

It was a sad wreck but a safe one. Stines later reported that the plane turned over so slowly that none of the passengers lost their positions. "It was," he said, "like rolling in a barrel."

Wien's employers, learning the bad news, wired that they would ship him another propeller by the first river boat. But Stines and the secretaries decided that they had had enough. They chose to make the rest of their journey by water. Keenly disappointed, Wien got permission from Fairbanks to complete the trip to Nome anyway.

When the new prop arrived, a few days later, he installed it and pointed the Fokker downhill toward a drop of only 400 feet. The take-off was close; the Fokker ploughed into brush and dropped almost to the river before it gained flying speed. The German engine, ill timed to the new propeller, vibrated badly as he headed westward. But he continued more than three hours, "juggling between strange peaks," and arrived at Nome safely—long before Stines did, he proudly points out.

Early in 1927 Noel and Ralph Wien left Fairbanks and founded their own airline, basing out of Nome. They borrowed money to buy one of Rodebaugh's old Standards and gave the Bering Sea town its first steady plane service. They were soon able to buy a second plane, a Stinson which had been brought to Alaska by the Wilkins expedition. Business was brisk; almost too brisk.

"A cordon of police may be necessary when Wien takes off," Nome's newspaper, the *Nugget,* reported one day. "There are six persons anxious to fly to Fairbanks, and the plane will not hold that many. There are two passengers for Candle and possibly a flight will be made to Kotzebue with diphtheria anti-toxin."

That winter Wien nearly lost his Stinson in a freakish accident. Landing at Lake Minchumina one late afternoon in December, he left his plane on the snow before the roadhouse and went to bed. He awoke during the night to the howl of high wind. Throwing on a parka, he hurried outdoors to check on his ship. There was nothing where it had stood but whirling snow.

The Stinson was gone!

The storm that had blown up so suddenly lasted for three days. Winds were so high that they swept the drifts from the lake till the surface was sheer ice.

Wien spent hour after anxious hour staring out the window for signs of his plane. The experience was like a ghost story. On the second day he saw the dim shape of the Stinson far out on the lake. Then snow began to fall more heavily, blotting it out. When the weather cleared briefly on the third day the plane was gone again!

At last the storm died down and he found his ship two miles away on the opposite shore, its "flippers" and propeller blades bent, its control rods and skis damaged.

He spent two days repairing it the best he could "with a monkey wrench and a blowtorch," and continued his journey toward Nome. The people there had suffered more than he from the accident. It had happened two days before Christmas, and Wien had all their gifts and mail on board.

The next year he was careful to make up for this disappointment, arriving at Nome on Christmas Eve with a full load of letters and packages. Children ran around his plane, jumping up and down with excitement. Old women wept. In their memory, the winter-locked town had never received any gifts at holiday-time. No town in Alaska appreciated air service more than Nome did the Wien brothers', especially in winter. Overland, it was a journey of several weeks by dog team to the nearest large town, and only essentials had been hauled.

In March, 1929, half a year before Eielson's journey to death, Wien made the first round trip by air between America and Asia. The reason for the flight, and the plane, were the same as in the case of Eielson. Wien had a contract to haul a load of furs from a vessel ice-bound off North Cape, Siberia, and he flew in the all-metal Hamilton in which Eielson was later to crash.

Wien's international journey caused a stir in Washington. The Assistant Secretary of Commerce wired him congratulations for a "most worthy pioneering effort." Wien shrugs his shoulders, remembering this acclaim. The spring sun was bright. "We just simply waited for clear and unlimited weather," he says, honestly, "and if we had run into a storm we would have turned back awfully fast."

He and his mechanic Calvin Cripe did have "a little trouble" on the return trip, he admits. The oil tank of the Hamilton, built into the leading edge of the wing, received no heat from the engine. He was cruising above the Siberian coast, over snow drifts much higher than any he had ever seen in Alaska, when the cap froze and pressure rose to a critical point.

The outside temperature that day was 50 below zero, but Mechanic Cripe opened the window and leaned out as far as he could into the biting blast. Just able to reach the vent, he punched it open with a knife.

It soon froze shut again.

Once more, he leaned out to open it. He had to repeat this almost insufferable task every ten or fifteen minutes during the six-hour flight.

"It was the mechanic," Wien says, "who deserved any congratulations for that trip."

Soon after his journey to Asia, Wien married Ada Bering Arthurs, the pretty, pale-complexioned, dark-haired daughter of the Nome postmaster. Later that year he sold his Nome company and made a long trip with his new wife to the United States. Returning, he formed another family outfit, flying out of Fairbanks, where his brother Sig joined him.

Today Wien Alaska Airlines has a large fleet of planes and fifty pilots, and a second generation of Wiens is taking to the air. Noel's son Merrill soloed on his sixteenth birthday and got his commercial, instrument and instrument instructor ratings when he was nineteen. He flew a while for the family outfit and for Pan American on its Alaska and Hawaii runs, then enlisted in the Air Force. His younger brother Richard is making bush flights for the family company and their cousin Bob, son of Ralph Wien, is doing likewise.

"Our boys," Mrs. Wien says, "were not handed their flying time or licenses, but had to earn and pay for all of it. Their first work was doing the lowliest and dirtiest tasks about the field. Of course, they did not want to work any place except around airplanes, even though they could get jobs elsewhere paying higher wages."

Noel Wien, during his distinguished career, has had many offers of work in the United States and Canada. He turned them all down, preferring to stay in Alaska.

"Alaska," he says, "keeps a fellow guessing. It tugs at you all the time. The States are too tame."

Wien hardly does justice to the Far North in words, but he has taken hundreds of photographs of the country's savage splendor. Many of Alaska's pilots have been amateur photographers but none of their albums rivals Wien's for artistic composition and imaginative choice of subject. Some of the shots, of crude flying fields and small towns, are precise and detailed; the ragged wind sock, the grassy turf of the runway, the piled oil cans and the battered planes are all shown for what they mean. Other shots, taken from the cockpit far aloft, give the most overwhelming impressions of wilderness and sky.

As Noel Wien stands in the library of his home, looking up at these photographs along the walls, he suddenly seems many miles and years distant.

"I remember when I took that picture," he'll say, softly. "I always liked Alaska . . . I rather liked to fly over the mountains . . . This country is intriguing in a way."

Chapter 6: JOE CROSSON
The Gallant Flyer

Joe Crosson, after Eielson, was Alaska's most famous pilot. Hero of the search for his lost comrade in 1929-30, he was also the talk of America for many other gallant "mercy" flights accomplished in time of disaster.

"Knight of the North," a United States newspaper once called him. "Angel in Furs," another. His name became even better known in later years when Pan American Airways entered Alaska, chose him as its chief pilot there and then made him the manager of its far-flung northern routes.

Crosson did not care for fame. A tall man with coal-black hair, a rugged build and a never-failing smile, he was as unassuming as he was warm-hearted. He shunned publicity. The term "mercy pilot" embarrassed him. Until he told the story of his flight for this book, shortly before his death, his wife complained that their three young sons had never heard it in full. She let them stay up long past midnight to listen.

Crosson grew up on a Kansas farm. He saw his first plane when he was eleven years old, at a county fair. He and his sister Marvel did not have the price of admission, so they watched the barnstormer's stunts from behind a fence.

"Joe grabbed my shoulders and jumped up and down," Marvel later remembered. "I'm going to be an aviator!" he shouted. "I'm going to be an aviator!"

Marvel, three years older than her brother, looked much like him, with coal-black hair and a flashing smile. She also shared his high ambition. Several years later, when the Crosson family moved to California, the two would-be pilots persuaded their parents to settle near San Diego, which had a busy airfield.

Joe got a job in a garage, Marvel in a camera store, and they saved up $150, enough to buy the motorless wreck of a Curtiss N-9 seaplane. Neighbors laughed when they set it up in their back yard. But Joe and his sister were serious. He ransacked junk yards for a long time until he had the parts to make a landplane of it.

He and Marvel then persuaded their parents to sell the family Ford, and bought a Curtiss OX-5 engine with the proceeds. They tried it out in the back yard. "It worked," Crosson later remembered, laughing, "too well! It blew all mother's chickens against a high board fence!"

At last the makeshift aircraft was ready to be towed to the airfield. Joe begged a friend who was an ex-Army pilot to give it a test. It took a lot of arguing, but the man, who knew that Joe was a clever mechanic, finally agreed.

The hop was a success.

"It flies! It flies!" brother and sister shouted in triumph. "It's ours! It's ours!"

They both soloed and barnstormed together in the years that followed, throughout the West. Joe said that he never enjoyed a trip as much as when Marvel was along. Then, in 1926, he heard that a pioneer company at Fairbanks, Alaska was looking for pilots. There was important work to be done up there, a friend told him. Aviation was just getting started, and there were no roads.

Joe liked the idea of a new country. He applied for a job and was hired by telegram. There was talk of Marvel's following him later, but their flying partnership was never resumed. After he left for the north she crashed to death in the Women's Air Derby in Arizona.

Crosson, when he arrived at Fairbanks, was "just a big kid," one Alaskan remembers, "with an embarrassed grin and only 500 hours in the air."

His first weeks in the north were a disappointment. The Fairbanks Company had no plane for him to fly. There had been too many accidents, his employers explained. Only one aircraft was in shape to operate, and a pilot named A. A. Bennett, who had arrived earlier, was flying that and in no mood to share it. Crosson went to work in a garage, repairing one of the wrecks.

Early one morning he lost patience, climbed into Bennett's ship, took it up and circled over town. It was good to be in the air again.

Bennett, hearing the engine, hurried out to the field and

stood on the runway angrily signalling for him to come back.

"Who do you think you are?" he shouted, as Crosson landed. "Get back to work and stay out of that ship!"

That was Crosson's first flight in Alaska.

It was not long, however, before he had a chance to make a real trip, in the same little Jenny, now much battered, that Ben Eielson had used for his first flights in 1923. His passenger was a miner named Van Curler, who wanted to fly seventy-five miles to his claim on the Upper Chena River. Van Curler assured Crosson that he had roughed out a "good airfield" there. Crosson was too new in Alaska to know what this might mean. As he arrived above the "airfield" he saw that it was "nothing but a potato patch, maybe 350 feet long, right in the middle of the river."

He shook his head. But Van Curler indignantly told him that Ben Eielson had once landed there "just fine." Deciding that he must meet this challenge, Crosson took the Jenny down. The landing confirmed his doubts. In his words: "I came down a little too short and hit the niggerheads. Wham! The ship turned over on its back."

Van Curler and all his groceries spilled out on the ground. His wife came hurrying toward the scene of the crash in a boat. Crosson was very disturbed, as he stood inspecting his upside-down plane. He had yet to learn that Alaska's frontier people were as casual about wrecks as they were about airfields.

"Don't you worry," the couple told him. "Did you ever see a Spanish windlass?"

Mrs. Van Curler fetched two poles and a length of cable. Her husband tied one end to the Jenny's tail, wound the other end around a stump, and started winding. The plane was part way over when the cable broke. They tried again. This time the scheme worked.

Crosson next discovered another catastrophe. The fuel had all spilled out of the tank. "Okay," said Van Curler, cheerfully, "we can fix that, too." He went to fetch ten gallons of lamp gas from his shed.

The steel propeller was bent, but this too was solved by the ingenious miner and his frontier wife. Mrs. Curler fetched a log from her woodpile.

"She held it behind the blade of the prop," Crosson recalled, "and we pounded the thing out to where it cleared the radiator of the engine. The top of the rudder was broken but I figured she'd still handle. The cabane struts were mashed clear over but the air was smooth and I thought the flying wires would hold okay.

"I got in and tried the engine. She was rough, but I let her wind up and took off. Oh boy, that old engine was really jumping around, but I wheeled in to Fairbanks careful as I could, landed, put the ship in a hangar, shut the doors and never told anyone."

Later that summer, flying a Waco, he took a miner named Joe Quigley to his cabin at Moose Creek—and had a still more violent meeting with the earth. The "airfield" to which Quigley proudly pointed was out of the question. "It was just a little knob. The only thing that could land there would be an eagle!" Crosson decided that it would be safer to use a nearby river bar.

In his words: "We sailed over a bunch of stumps and hit. The gravel was hard as pavement. I no more than touched when I saw that I was going to run into the river, so I poured on the coal. But the Waco slowed up and rapidly ended in the water, stuck on its nose just slightly upside down at a forty-five degree angle—in those days a favorite position."

Quigley was hurt. His nose, torn against a strut, was bleeding badly. His wife, who came running to the scene, took one look at him, ran to fetch her first aid kit, and proceeded to sew up the wound. There was, however, no way of mending the plane. New parts were needed to repair the crankcase and the propeller. Crosson started out on foot to the nearest settlement, eighty-five miles away.

"You may think the trail is tough," Mrs. Quigley told him, "but don't you leave it, or you'll be a goner."

For four days he ploughed through soggy mud, sometimes knee deep, before he reached the settlement, a road and an automobile. He later returned to the Quigleys' cabin with a second pilot in another plane. This time he landed on a longer river bar, six miles away. The two of them lugged the parts through the brush, repaired the Waco and flew both planes back to their base. "That," Crosson summed up, smiling, "was the end of that little trip."

As it turned out, this rough and tumble accident, early in his career, was one that he never forgot. It was the only occasion in more than 8,000 hours of flying on which Crosson ever caused an injury to a passenger.

His apprenticeship had hardly begun. The pioneer pilots of Alaska, it was said, spent more time "hiking out" from wilderness wrecks than they spent flying. Crosson learned that this was more than a joke. His first year in the Far North was a constant contest with crude runways—and also with faulty engines.

The small, water-cooled Hispano-Suizas which powered the Fairbanks fleet in 1926 gave the pilots endless trouble. "Every time we made a trip we'd have to pull the bank and grind the valves," Crosson said. No matter how often these engines were overhauled, they would boil over and quit in the air.

The "Hissos" were undependable enough in summer. Later that year Crosson learned what it meant to fly with them in freeze-up time and winter. In one month's time, he worked a total of 30 hours in the air, crashed three times, and spent twenty days waiting for rescue or hiking back to civilization.

This chain of misadventures began one bleak November morning as he was cruising in a "Hisso"-powered Standard at 6,000 feet above the Toklat River. One of the engine's wrist pins broke; "Clank, clank, clank, she kept turning over, but she sounded like she would fall to pieces." He hastily brought the plane down on the smoothest looking river bar he could see and came to a jarring stop among the boulders.

He spent the rest of the day trying to repair the engine. It was hopeless. The connecting rod was broken, and new parts were needed. When dusk fell over the wilds he built a fire of driftwood, drank some soup, wrapped himself in a blanket and stretched out under the wing of the plane. But he could not sleep. He heard animals moving through the brush along the riverbank. A circle of flashing eyes formed around him in the dark. Terrified, he bounded into his plane and spent the rest of the night cramped in the small cabin.

He woke the next morning to the first snowfall of the year, and decided to hike to a roadhouse he had seen from the air, shortly before landing—some twelve miles away. His roundsoled flying boots slipped in the soft snow. The whirling flakes blinded him. He had not been walking long when he fell down a steep bank, painfully wrenching his knee. For one terrible moment, he thought he had broken his leg. "There I was in the snowstorm all alone and nobody knew where I was at!"

Finding that he could still walk, he braced himself with a stick and limped along, feeling his way with every step, during the brief daylight hours and for some time into the night. He was forced to break trail through a dense undergrowth of willow and spruce, climbing over logs, detouring around wide sloughs and beaver ponds, as he followed the main bank of the stream to the roadhouse.

His hike had hardly begun. The next morning he started along a rough trail toward Kobe, the nearest small station on the Alaska Railroad. Old-timers at the roadhouse told him to avoid all lakes, as they were not yet frozen solid, but when he came to a large, icy stretch "nice, smooth, easy walking," he could not resist it. He'd gone some distance when he drew back, horrified, just in the nick of time, before a great gaping hole. There were tracks on the other side. A dog sled must have crashed through here, man and team drowning below!

He hurried back to shore, and detoured around all the lakes in his path, his blistered feet hurting more and more, till he arrived at a small Indian settlement. The Indians gave him the bad news that the Nenana River, eight miles beyond, had not yet frozen over for the winter. One, however, offered to take him across the torrent by boat. The man led out his dog team; "nine, nice, strong, big Huskies." Crosson stepped eagerly aboard the sled.

"No, no!" the Indian shouted. "My dogs too green!"

He yelped to his animals and rode swiftly away down the trail. Crosson stumbled after him, mile after mile, to the river. The crossing was another ordeal. The roaring river was full of crashing ice cakes. The Indian's boat was made of mooseskin, ribbed only with willow branches, and no more than nine feet long. Crosson crouched astonished beside the native as he deftly worked a double-ended paddle, steering between the ice cakes, to the opposite shore.

"I couldn't take one breath all the way over," the celebrated Alaska airman later admitted. "I was never so terrified as in that wobbly little gadget!"

He limped the rest of the way to the railroad and took the next train back to Fairbanks.

"How is the airplane?" his employer barked. "What was the delay? Where the devil have you been?"

There was rush work to be done, he said. Crosson left Fairbanks immediately, in a new Swallow, on another ill-starred trip.

This time he nearly lost his life. He was taking off with two passengers from a river bar near McGrath. "We had just reached the end of the bar when the motor began to spit. Then she quit cold. The Swallow crashed.

"The water rushed all around us and for a minute I thought we were floating down the river. Then I realized the ship was on her back. Everything but the cockpit and the leading edge of the wing was under water—but we were high and dry! The Swallow had flopped onto a little sandbar right in the middle of the stream!"

It had been a remarkable stroke of luck. He and his passengers climbed out and huddled beside the plane, helplessly watching as ice cakes smashed against it. Crosson was in despair. At any moment, the new Swallow might be knocked from its precarious perch into the torrent and swept away!

Villagers who had heard the crash came running along the river bank. Among them was an old-timer with a team of horses. "We'll use a rope!" he shouted, across the roar of the stream, "and pull the plane to shore!"

The rope was hastily stretched across the river and tied to the Swallow's landing gear. The horses moved ahead; a cry of disappointment rose from the crowd as the landing gear broke away. Crosson and his helpers pushed the plane over onto its belly and tied the rope to the tail. Once more the horses struggled forward. The Swallow would not budge.

A third try was made, with a pole under each wing for leverage. As Crosson described it: "We got the cockeyed thing into the water and waded in clear up to our necks. We heaved. The horses heaved. Suddenly the plane hopped up onto the bank. Her tail was off. Her wings were all in pieces. All that was left of the company's new Swallow was the motor!"

There was now no plane left for Crosson to fly but the old Standard that he had left on the Toklat river bar. As soon as he returned to Fairbanks he set forth with a mechanic to salvage it. Another pilot delivered them to the scene of his forced landing and they spent four days repairing the first damage and also mending the elevators, which had been battered on the ground by winds.

Crosson took off, counting on better luck this trip. He had been in the air only ten minutes when the oil pressure dropped to zero. He brought the Standard down on a frozen pond, removed and cleaned the oil screen, took off again. Once more fallen pressure forced the plane to earth. Once more, he tried the air. Five times, in all, he was forced to land.

On the sixth try the engine began to miss.

Crosson landed on another lake and he and his mechanic worked several hours repairing the engine. By this time they had had enough of dropping oil pressure. They decided to cut a hole through the fire wall so that the mechanic could reach through from the cabin and pour oil into the tank to keep the plane in the air.

They took off again. The Standard had just gained flying speed when flames blazed in the cockpit!

Crosson skilfully sideslipped the plane down onto the snow and helped his mechanic to safety, just in the nick of time. The tanks exploded. The two men stood in the wild forest and watched the blaze of the aircraft as thick smoke filled the air. "There was nothing we could do. That was the end of that ship!"

This time Crosson had no river to guide him. He and his mechanic were deep in the woods. They floundered for hours, till Crosson got his bearings by climbing a tree. Hiking on, they reached the Kuskokwim River and stood debating a while on the steep bank. How were they going to cross to the roadhouse on the other shore? There was no bridge. There was no boat. The freeze-up, by this time, had plugged the mighty stream but the slushy surface still seemed too soft for walking.

Crosson decided to fell a large tree, which reached half way across. One at a time he and his mechanic crawled out along it, dragging two long poles. Then, leaning their weight on the poles, they stepped carefully over the mushy surface and managed to reach the opposite shore.

They finally arrived back at Fairbanks, after another long and exhausting hike, three weeks after they had left it on what was to have been a routine trip.

Despite all these harrowing adventures, Crosson had no thought of returning to California. He was already part of the frontier, liking its forthright, air-minded people, drawn by the challenge of the country, impatient to go on with his new work. Only a few months later he flew all the way from Fairbanks to Barrow, crossing the 500 miles of forbidding wilds which only Eielson and Wilkins had crossed before him.

He made the flight in bitter subzero weather in another small Swallow, powered with another of the "Hisso" engines!

There was much of bravado in Crosson's journey. He set out on three hours notice, taking along a rag doll as a mascot. The Wilkins expedition had arrived at Fairbanks and was about to proceed to Barrow for its second year of work. Wilkins and Eielson did not have room aboard their ship for a reporter, A. M. Smith, who wanted to go with them. Smith wanted to charter a local plane and Crosson agreed to make the trip.

The Fairbanks-Barrow route was hardly one for the Swallow. The open-cockpit plane not only had the most tempermental of engines, but a perilously low fuel range for the trip. There was no heat in the Swallow; just some flexible tubes hooked onto the engine exhaust which a Fairbanks mechanic had hastily installed "so Joe at least could warm his feet."

Wilkins and Eielson, warning him of the dangers of the route, advised him to fly ahead of them 200 miles to the Arctic village of Wiseman and refuel. Then, it was agreed, they would arrive over Wiseman in their larger plane, and he could follow them the rest of the way north.

Crosson arrived at Wiseman on schedule, but his "Hisso" engine was already up to the usual tricks. The radiator had frozen and broken. As he was working hastily on the runway, trying to repair it, the Wilkins plane arrived and circled overhead. Not wishing to delay the expedition, Crosson motioned Wilkins and Eielson on.

Now he would have to make the long journey to the top of the continent, with an engine that had failed him so often, on his own.

He took his engine to the Wiseman roadhouse and spent most of the day repairing it with a soldering iron. The next morning he cheerfully told his passenger he was ready to proceed.

Experts consider this flight of Crosson's one of the most remarkable in the history of Alaskan aviation. With only an old ship's compass and a crude map to guide him (the same map that had nearly brought Eielson and Wilkins to disaster the year before), he found the way. He trusted his "Hisso" through the canyons of the awesome Endicott Mountains, and luckily it did not fail him. He followed the icy reel of the Anaktuvuk River to its confluence with the mighty Colville and then struck out over the snowy flats beyond.

By this time his compass was altogether worthless; it had shaken loose from its mounting and dropped to one side. He navigated by the light of the dim sun, judging his position by the shadow of the struts on the Swallow's wing. Reaching the shore line fifty miles east of Barrow, he followed it around, through flurries of snow.

It was nearly dark, and there were only a few gallons of gas left in the Swallow's tank, when he sighted the farthest-north town and landed his passenger at his destination. The ground temperature was 40 below zero.

Exhilarated, Crosson decided to return to Fairbanks by a new route. He wanted to explore, see some more strange country. Two days later, in a calm between snow squalls, he left Barrow alone and started south along the Arctic coast, over empty, snow-covered shores which no man but the crew of the dirigible *Norge* had ever seen from the air. Only a few Eskimo settlements broke the lonely expanse over which he must fly, and they were far between. Few white men had ever visited this part of Alaska.

For three hours, the Swallow soared on its precarious course above great drifted snow banks and towering pressure ridges.

Then the Hisso engine began to boil.

Crosson put the plane into a long, slow glide and managed to reach the smooth surface of a lagoon. Steam rushed out as he removed the cap. He filled a can with fine ice chips and poured them into the leader tank. During this time he left the "Hisso" running, fearing that he would not be able to start it again alone.

Climbing back into the cockpit, he had barely touched the throttle when the Swallow astonished him by shooting forward on the slick ice so fast that it had crossed most of the lagoon before he could get it into the air.

Snow filled the sky, as he continued his lonely journey. A full-scale blizzard was blowing up ahead. He managed to skirt the edge of it, and arrived in the nick of time at the coastal Eskimo village of Kotzebue. The startled Eskimos came running through the falling snow and crowded around the Swallow. They laughed and laughed, Crosson said, at their first sight of an airplane.

When the storm cleared, four days later, he started out again, heading inland toward Fairbanks, and followed the Kobuk River to the town of Noorvik. There, as he landed on rough river ice, the right landing gear strut was broken. An Eskimo boy who had never before seen a plane begged him to let him repair it. Crosson watched as the boy ingeniously sawed splinters from a plank, fitted them to the strut and wrapped around some "babish." The strut held perfectly, he said, all the way home, and a long time afterward.

The last lap of Crosson's remarkable journey was the worst in terms of weather. Nearing his home base, he flew into a blizzard so thick that he barely managed, by flying low above a river and the railroad track, to make his way to the Fairbanks field.

In the smallest plane ever to fly far into the Alaskan Arctic, Crosson had made, in all, a 1,580-mile circuit over strange territory. With a "Hisso" engine!

The rag doll mascot had proven a good one. The bold trip, which Crosson had made so nonchalantly, almost gaily, was to prove a turning point of his career. It lifted him out of the ranks of the bush pilots into the world's small, select group of flying explorers.

Wilkins and Eielson were much impressed. Recognizing Crosson's caliber, they invited him to join their Antarctic expedition the following year, and he flew with them into the south polar regions.

Crosson and Eielson became firm friends. The earnest pioneer and the gay one spent long hours talking about polar aviation. Eielson exercised a strong influence on Crosson, and when he returned to Alaska in 1929 to launch an airline for the Aviation Corporation Crosson went to work as one of his pilots.

Ironically, it was Eielson's tragic death that catapulted Crosson to fame, then fortune. The whole world heard of Crosson's dauntless and finally successful efforts to find his lost comrade in the dark storms of that violent winter. In the years that followed Crosson, more than any other one man, took Eielson's place, working to realize his vision of large-scale air service in the Far North.

Pan American Airways, buying Eielson's company in 1932 and merging it with local outfits, named Crosson as chief pilot. First major U.S. operator to enter the Far North, Pan American spent millions of dollars and brought Alaska its first fleet of radio-equipped multi-engine transports, its first flight communications system, its first airline in the usual sense of the word. "Big silver ships" came to the north and Crosson and the other pilots wore trim Pan American uniforms.

It was a big change for a bush pilot accustomed to wrecking Swallows on sand bars. Still, it was pioneer work. Pan American, which had always before flown southern, warmweather routes, found Crosson's help invaluable, and in 1937 promoted him to manager of the Alaska run. Through him, the airline tapped a pool of technical skills that it could not have hired in the United States at any price. He hired bush pilots who knew the country, to help choose the best field and station sites. Veteran Alaska mechanics were also hired to winterize the fleet, warm the oil, protect the engines, cover the wings. It was all an old story to Crosson; once, weary of scraping frost from aircraft wings, he had personally made the first wing cover in the north, from a length of bed-sheeting.

He had less and less chance to fly in his Pan American post. In the summer of 1935, however, when the beloved humorist Will Rogers crashed to death near Barrow with round-the-world Pilot Wiley Post, it was he who hurried to the top of the continent in a small float plane, and then rushed their bodies back to the United States.

Once more, his name was headlined throughout the world for gallant work in time of tragedy. His flight caused such a stir that a move was made in Washington to award him the Congressional Medal of Honor and the Distinguished Flying Cross.

He refused these decorations. Hearing of the proposed honors, he told Alaska's Delegate in Congress that he would not accept them. "The whole idea of medals was quite unwarranted," he said, flatly. "Not at all in keeping with what I did."

Crosson, accompanied by a flight mechanic, had flown from Fairbanks to Barrow as soon as he had heard of the fatal crash. Fog had hung low over the Barrow lagoon as he left there at midnight with his death-load on the return trip. His small float plane, heavily weighted with extra fuel for emergency, had ploughed up onto a sand bar the first time he tried to take off. During the journey bad weather had driven him far off course, and he had been forced down on an Arctic lake to refuel.

Altogether, Crosson had flown a total of thirteen hours in a nineteen-hour period to bring home the bodies of Rogers and Post. But this sad and exhausting journey, he felt, was no more than that of an Eskimo who had run twelve miles across the tundra to take the first news of the crash to Barrow. Why not honor the Eskimo, he asked? His flight, he insisted, was one that any of Alaska's pioneers would have made in the course of his work.

Two years later, when a Soviet pilot, Sigismund Levanevsky, was lost on an attempted hop over the North Pole from Moscow to California, Crosson left his desk to do another job of rushed, gallant flying. Levanevsky had made his last position report two hours south of the Pole on the Alaska side, and there was a chance that he could have crashed on American soil.

Here was a chance for American flyers to repay their debt for Soviet help in the search for Eielson. Many pilots including Wilkins took part in the futile search, which lasted for many months. Crosson was one of the first to act. As soon as he heard that the Russian plane was missing he organized a three-way hunt in Pan American planes. He himself took the hardest job, heading north in an Electra over the tundra, circling out over the Arctic Ocean and returning over the peaks of the Endicotts. He personally scanned a total of 80,000 square miles before returning to Fairbanks.

Crosson got much publicity for this "mercy" flight, and as usual did not appreciate it. The youngest Division Manager in Pan American's world system, he was also without question the most unassuming. In 1941, after Pan American started service between the United States and Alaska, his headquarters were moved to Seattle. A capable executive of hardy poise, he still talked the rough grammar of the frontier. His secretaries could never break him of the habit of answering his own phone. He was never too busy to see an old trapper or a new pilot.

He built a remarkably loyal airline organization for Pan

American. The pilots would do anything for this pioneer who knew their problems backwards and forwards and faced them as his own. The entire staff worked unusually hard for Crosson, respecting him as men always respect an employer who has earned his title the hard way.

He also served the Army well. When the first squadron of military planes was ordered north shortly before the war, an operations manual prepared under his direction served as a kind of Bible for the pilots. His knowledge of Alaska flying proved a precious asset to the Air Force, which borrowed him from Pan American during the war to help solve technical problems.

Crosson resigned from Pan American in 1944. The last years of his life were shadowed by illness. His doctors forbade him to fly any more. He went to work at the Seattle airfield, managing a plane and parts supply business serving the Far North.

"Always," he said, "in some way, I want to be part of aviation in Alaska."

In 1949 he died at the airfield of a heart attack, after two decades of selfless work in the field which he and Eielson had chosen to make their own.

Chapter 7: **HAROLD GILLAM**

Ace of Storms

There was never another flyer in the Far North like Harold
Gillam, the little fellow who, with Crosson, was the hero of
the Eielson search.

"Thrill 'em, spill 'em, no kill 'em Gillam," people called him
in the years that followed. Some seasoned air travelers were
known to climb out of his plane at way stops and refuse to go
on with him. There were others who said that his skill was
superhuman, and liked to fly with no one else.

He was a pilot who astounded other pilots, even the pilots of
Alaska, by his bold contempt for fog and storm.

There were three kinds of weather, old-timers say, in the
day before airways were built. There was the "airline weather"
that cautious Pan American Airways would fly: "clear and unlimited." There was the whole gamut of good, bad and indiffer-
ent weather that most of the bush pilots flew. And there was
"Gillam weather."

The others made a grim joke of it. Hearing that he was up in a bad storm, they would claim double reason for cancelling out their flights. "Don't believe I'll try it," they would say. "God's plenty busy taking care of Gillam."

He was a legend from one end of Alaska to the other. "He thought he could beat the elements." The other pioneers, in that era of "contact" flight, were past-masters at skirting and testing storms; dodging their way over, under and between fog banks; fighting for sight of the earth, and making forced landings if they lost it. Only on mercy trips, where the lives of passengers were at stake, did they fly "blind" very far.

Gillam would bore his way through blinding weather on the most routine trips as if he were a modern instrument pilot flying a radio beam.

In 1943, he lost his battle with the elements. But for more than ten years he flew all over the frontier without seeming to give a hoot for nature's mood.

Nobody quite understood how he did it.

Gillam had a brooding look. Burly, broad-shouldered, he gave an impression of suppressed power. He had once been an amateur boxer, and looked the part. His coal-black eyes peered out from heavy, overhanging eyebrows. He was swarthy, of Irish descent. There was a rumor that he had Indian blood in him.

He never laughed. Obsessed by aviation, he would sometimes join a technical argument. Most of the time he was silent, and shunned the company of other pilots. "How's the weather?" they would ask, as he landed. "Not bad," he would tell them. Always, with a dead-pan expression, "not bad." That was all.

He was a mysterious fellow. For a long time, he kept two

polar bears in a cage beside his hangar. No one at the airfield understood why, least of all his mechanic, who had to chase them up and down the runway whenever they broke loose. Gillam never paid any attention to them. He'd just flown them in one day from a trip and ordered them kept there. He never discussed his actions, trivial or important, with anyone. Mechanics who worked with Gillam for years say that they never had any inkling of what was on his mind. Women liked him.

Son of an auto salesman, Gillam grew up at Chadron, Nebraska. He ran away from home at the age of sixteen, joined the Navy, and spent several years in the Pacific aboard a destroyer. Mustered out in 1923, he went to work in Seattle, as a painter. He was soon bored. One day he saw a sign in an American Legion hall, advertising for construction workers in Alaska. He took the next boat north.

He spent a while operating power shovels and tractors. Joe Crosson's first recollection of Gillam was of a husky kid bumping along in a tractor smoothing the surface of the Fairbanks airfield. After this job Gillam used to hang around the field, dourly watching the planes. One day he told Crosson he believed he would learn to fly.

As a student, he escaped death in the Far North's first fatal air crash. He was riding with an instructor in a two-place Swallow when the ship slid out of control and spun to earth. The instructor died of his injuries. Gillam, badly gashed in the head and hands, refused to stay in the hospital. Before the doctor had the stitches out of his wounds, he was in the air again. Soon he was practicing spins alone.

Few men have ever had as much right to call themselves

"natural-born" flyers. When he made his extraordinary trip to Asia, during the search for Eielson, he had not even qualified, as yet, for a pilot's license. Crosson was astonished when this cocky fledgling, burrowing blind through fog and storm, beat him to the *Nanuk*. Other pilots attached to the expedition, men of longer experience, were embarrassed when the young novice became, with Crosson, the hero of the search. Gillam applied for a license, after the search was over, and failed the routine government test. The inspector, knowing his reputation, only laughed and certified him anyway as an airman.

The first three years of Gillam's work as a bush pilot were reckless ones. He chose the foggiest, windiest, rainiest part of the mainland to fly in: the mountain region of the southeast coast. Only the Aleutian Islands have worse year-round weather. Hauling passengers and freight to copper mines back of the seaport of Cordova, he cracked up one plane after another.

Nothing seemed to faze him. A pilot named Oscar Winchell, who worked for him a while during these years, was both frightened and amazed. Winchell tells of one flight when he and Gillam were speeding through a narrow pass in windy weather, thick fog boiling all around them. The plane rose and sank violently. The rolling fog got more and more blinding. Gillam reached a valley where he could have turned back while the turning was good. He flew on.

"He was just as cool about it," Winchell says, "as a doctor goin' to make an operation. Nothin' seemed to register. He set there smokin' a cigarette. Once he tipped a wing to show me a moose close by on the mountainside. He just seemed to know he was goin' to make it—and he did."

He was a stern man to work for, Winchell says. On another

hair-raising flight the two of them were circling at 16,000 feet above a sea of cloud, with almost no gas left in the tank. They knew that an airfield, cradled by mountains, lay hidden below. But there was no break in the fog.

"He was settin' there," Winchell remembers, "with not a worry on his face. We circled and circled. Then he just pulled the throttle and took her down. We could see a little, then she was too thick again. We were comin' down blind right in the mountains!

"Then we broke out in the clear—just over the airfield!

"He landed and climbed out.

"I said: 'Aren't you gonna taxi over to the hangar?'

"He said: 'No, we'll tie her down right here.'

"I said: 'Wouldn't it be better to taxi her over to the hangar out of the wind?'

"He told me: 'I *said* we'll leave her here.'

"I looked at the gas gauge and I understood. It showed empty. Not a drop left! He didn't say nothin' more, just took his grip and started walkin' to town."

Even for a careful pilot, the wind-buffeted runways of the copper mine region were risky ones. At Cordova Gillam had to use a small lake surrounded by craggy peaks. Near one of the mines there was no better place than a narrow clearing on top of a sheer bluff; so narrow, Winchell says, that "if you undershot you ran into the bluff. And when you took off you hadn't a foot of spare."

These so-called airfields were dangerous enough by daylight. But Gillam did not always fly by daylight. As often as not, during those first reckless years, he would sleep in the morning till noon and then fly late into the night.

"For some reason," Winchell says, "he seemed to like to fly in the dark. He would have got killed, but I think he had abnormally sharp eyes. I always grabbed a flashlight to walk from the field to a roadhouse, but he would never bother. He'd step along on a pitch-black night, as sure-footed as a wild animal."

One night people at the town of Copper heard the roar of Gillam's engine and ran to their cabin windows. His Swallow, its navigation lights flashing against the hill, was circling to land in the darkness.

Men hurried down the trail to mark off the field with lanterns. Gillam did not bother to wait for their help. His ship, heavily loaded with ore concentrates, crashed and rolled over an embankment. A large stump tore through the windshield, missing him only by inches.

One day a trader at Copper, "Honest John" McCreary, fell down cellar and ran a nail through his stomach. Just before dusk, an Indian knocked at the door of Gillam's cabin. "McCreary die," he said.

Gillam flew the groaning man 125 miles through darkness and driving snow to the nearest doctor, at the town of Kennecott. When the doctor told him that the patient might not last till morning, he took off again, close to midnight, and flew another 200 miles in his small plane to fetch McCreary's son at Cordova.

As he landed there on the small, frozen lake a wheel broke through the ice. The ship sagged over, sinking part way into the water, and a spar of the lower right wing was cracked. It took three hours for Gillam and his helpers to hoist the plane out and drag it to the end of the lake for take-off. A gloomy group watched as he poured gas into the tank.

"You taking off, Harold?" someone asked, "with that busted spar?"

"Ice is awful thin," said somebody else.

"Oh, it's okay," Gillam tersely told them, as he screwed on the cap. I think it'll be all right."

He motioned his passenger in, took off over the "rubber" ice and returned to Kennecott in the hours before dawn. McCreary, as it happened, lived. Whether he had lived or died, it was all in a night's work to Gillam.

He wrecked so many planes in the copper mine region that after three years he decided to call it quits, and moved to Fairbanks for a new try. Suddenly his luck, or his flying, changed. Borrowing money for a second-hand Pilgrim, he flew it for many months without so much as scratching it. Soon he had earned enough to buy two more Pilgrims. He refused to have license numbers painted on these new planes, nor would he let his mechanic letter them with the Gillam Airways name. The mechanic believes this was because he was superstitious, after so many close calls.

The surprising fact is that from this time on, until his death, Gillam never wrecked another plane.

This does not mean that he had no accidents at all. Such a record was, of course, unheard of in Alaska. Once he lost his way and ran out of gas, in foggy weather, deep in the wild tundra country between Fairbanks and Barrow. He landed safely and was rescued by Eskimos with dog teams after four days. They found him wearing coveralls and bedroom slippers, hunched in the cockpit as off-hand as if he were waiting in a hotel room for a telephone call. The temperature was forty below zero!

Another time he ran out of gas, circling to land at the town of

Anchorage, and brought his plane, on wheels, down on the half-frozen inlet beside the town. Poker-faced, he helped his passengers out onto an ice floe. Boats arrived to the rescue, and the plane was towed to shore.

A third time he damaged a plane landing on rough ice at an Arctic coast town. He repaired it and flew on.

These were the most serious mishaps he had in eight years of the boldest flying, year in and year out, that the Far North has ever known. It was also spectacularly useful flying. Gillam's air work now entered a brilliant phase.

In the winter of 1936 he made a series of experimental, high-altitude hops for the United States Weather Bureau. The government in that year knew little about the temperature and humidity of the air masses above Alaska. Such data was sorely needed to improve weather forecasts not only within Alaska itself but also, as America's weather strikes mostly from the north, throughout all of Canada and the United States. Gillam risked his neck to get it.

Each day, at dawn and dusk, he took off from the Fairbanks field, carrying recording equipment in his plane. Spiraling to an altitude of 17,000 feet, he then returned in precise circles to earth. Later, with modern aircraft and ground aids, such weather hops were to become routine. In that year, accomplished strictly "contact" in Gillam's small Pilgrim, they could be considered safe only in good weather. Seldom did any kind of storm or fog cause him to miss a flight.

He made many of the hops virtually blind. His mechanic would stand outside their shack hangar on the field and talk to him by radio, bringing him down as best he could by the sound of the engine. But this scheme was hardly windproof.

"You're west of town!" the mechanic yelled, one stormy day.

"I'm headed east all the time," Gillam barked.

"You're still west, Harold!" the mechanic shouted. "You're drifting out of earshot!"

The Pilgrim was blown twelve miles beyond the town limits, and Gillam, still descending blind, broke out into sight of earth just in time to swerve, missing a small mountain called Ester Dome by only a few feet.

Once his banking ship terrified Fairbanks by roaring down over the very center of town, just missing the power company smokestack. The plane was so close that witnesses saw the flash of the smokestack's red obstruction lights on its silver wings!

This close call was apparently too much even for Gillam. He installed a direction finder in his Pilgrim for the rest of his weather hops. A battery charge was used as a homing device at the airfield. It was the first such installation in Alaska.

The next year Gillam turned to another, equally remarkable job. It was that summer that the Soviet pilot Sigismund Levanevsky was lost on his flight over the North Pole. A Soviet rescue party, equipped with an airplane and an ice-breaker, arrived at Barrow for the search, and needed fuel and other supplies from Fairbanks to carry on its work. Gillam agreed to do the freighting, and flew doggedly back and forth all summer over the dangerous Fairbanks-Barrow route in his small Pilgrim. "Flying for the Russians," Alaskans say, "Harold Gillam wore that air route smooth."

It was his navigation that mystified other flyers. In their opinion, he was flirting with disaster on each trip he made. The flight from Fairbanks to Barrow took six and a half hours, with favorable winds. He carried fuel for only seven. Everybody knew how difficult it was to find the pinpoint town at the top of the continent, even in good weather. There was a great deal of fog that summer. Gillam, time and again, would leave Fairbanks, fly much of the long journey "on top," and then come down to land at Barrow through murk that "not even a seagull could land in."

A United Airlines pilot named Danneld Cathcart, who happened to be visiting Alaska that summer, flew with Gillam on one of these freighting trips and reported that he found it hard to believe what he had seen with his own eyes. Gillam, he said, climbed to a high altitude after leaving Fairbanks and flew for nearly seven hours above a sea of unbroken fog. Then, suddenly, without the least hesitation, he nosed the plane down, blind.

Cathcart saw nothing, either vertically or horizontally, until a house and some antennae poles flashed by the windows as Gillam landed the plane on the Barrow lagoon.

Barrow, in this year, had a radio station, but its weather reports would have kept most pilots away. "We are always worried," says Stanley Morgan, the local Weather Officer, who watched all Gillam's landings that summer. "The antennae poles were within 500 feet of the runway. The Eskimos would stand in line and light flares, but often the fog was so thick he couldn't see them. Sometimes we'd try to direct him down by radio. Other times he'd just come down on his own. Once he couldn't have seen the ice till the moment he landed. And he hadn't enough gas, that time, to taxi his ship to shore. I frankly don't know how he did it."

Gillam seemed to prefer a daring job to any other. He sought such jobs. He set his next difficult assignment for himself, the following year, and made history.

Ben Eielson, in 1924, had been the first pilot to fly the United States mail in the Far North. Gillam, in 1938, was the first to fly it on schedule. The Post Office Department had not asked him to do so. His contract merely called for service to twenty Kuskokwim River towns. When Pan American Airways had previously handled the route, people had had no idea when their mail might arrive. Gillam resolved to make his stops as punctual as clockwork. Month in and month out, he did so, and with a perfect safety record.

Landing often at the little wayposts on thin ice or deep-drifted snow, he never once damaged his Pilgrims. No kind of weather stopped him. He seemed to have developed a sixth sense.

Other pilots still like to tell the story of the day he came into McGrath. Snow whitened the windows of the roadhouse, that late winter afternoon. The panes rattled with wind. Huddled beside the big Yukon stove, a large group of restless flyers were settling down to their twentieth round of poker. For three days, they had been grounded by a blizzard. "Really a storm," one remembers. "I wouldn't have whipped a cat out there that night."

They heard the engine faintly, at first, over the wind's roar. Then the noise was loud overhead. Leaving their game, the pilots crowded to the windows. They could not see it yet, but there was a plane up there, coming in blind to land. Nobody wondered who was flying it. Any man in the room would have staked his chips it was Gillam.

The sound of the engine traveled back and forth, louder and louder, until it seemed that the plane would crash into the roof. Then the blurred shape of Gillam's lighted single-engine Pilgrim shot into view. Just over the runway and exactly in line with it, it ploughed to a stop in the deep drifts.

Gillam, bundled heavily in furs, unloaded the mail sacks for McGrath and came plodding casually through the snow.

"Will you gas me up, Charlie?" he asked the old-time McGrath mechanic. "I'll be going right on to Fairbanks."

He asked for a cup of coffee and stood alone as he drank it, silent, warming his back against the stove. He opened the door to see if the mechanic had finished, slammed it shut. He stood a moment, hands in pockets, watching the poker game. Then he walked out without saying a word.

As they heard him taxi down the runway, the other pilots crowded once more to the windows. A ring of brightness broke the snow-filled dusk; Gillam had turned up his landing lights for take-off. All eyes followed the Pilgrim as it came roaring back—and slowed to a sputtering stop. "By golly," said the mechanic. "Don't believe Harold can make it. Snow must be over two foot deep."

Gillam tried again and failed. Then he walked back and asked the mechanic to get out a tractor. "Make a path just wide enough for the wheels," he said. "That'll be okay." He sat alone in his plane as the chugging cat broke a runway. Then he gunned the engine and was gone.

One of the pilots in the roadhouse turned up the radio receiver, as they went back to their game. All evening they heard no position report from Gillam. There was nothing but static and zero-zero weather reports. The men began to worry. Could it be possible that Gillam was in trouble? Should they go out and search?

They decided to send a query to Fairbanks. The return news both relieved and annoyed them. Gillam had landed there on schedule, as he always landed on schedule. He had crossed 300 miles of wilderness through the heavy snowstorm by night, so little concerned that he had not even bothered to use his radio.

Washington officials report that his Kuskokwim delivery was one of the most perfect in the history of the United States mails anywhere, even compared to service by land or water transport. The record is marked in his log-book in proud, extremely neat printing: a cross before each date, and a hand-written entry at the top of the page, "Cross-sign indicates all stops Kuskokwim mail route." But only the people in the villages could testify what this meant. Trappers and traders could almost set their watches by the coming and going of his silver Pilgrim. "To-day's Gillam day. Better finish that letter. Time to go out and meet the ship."

Sometimes he flew the mail route high, barreling down through fog or storm to make his stops. More often he flew it low, just level with the treetops, as he followed twisting river bends. If his ski-plane were forced too low, he would land and taxi along on the ice. Once, determined to keep his schedule, he taxied this way along the river for ten miles!

As the years passed, Gillam earned a reputation of being "part bird." But his mechanic, a ruddy-cheeked, practical man named Tom Appleton, gives some more down-to-earth reasons for his legendary skill. He says that Gillam worked harder at flying than most people realized. "He didn't proceed by guess and by gosh. Harold had a scientific mind. He was always figuring and plotting." He bought many books on meteorology, Appleton says, and studied the weather thoroughly. He also installed some of Alaska's first primitive air-ground stations on his routes, hiring old-timers at the roadhouses to tend them.

Very early, he began to work with instruments. In 1936, the year of his weather hops, he began draping a hood around the cockpit and trying to fly "by the panel." Long before most of the bush pilots, he sent to the United States for a directional gyro, a sensitive altimeter and an artificial horizon, and installed them in his Pilgrims.

"Gillam had a theory," Appleton says, "that the weather is never as bad as it looks." Instruments allowed him to test the theory when others would not have dared. But this does not entirely explain his uncanny record. Every pilot knows that there is nothing more dangerous than a mixture of "contact" and half-way instrument techniques. Gillam had, after all, no radio beams to follow in those early years. His Pilgrims, which had no de-icing equipment, were hardly planes for instrument flight in any case. And there was always the unknown and unpredictable factor of winds.

Even Appleton was mystified by Gillam's performance. Other pilots were amazed that he could make such a gamble, over and over and over again. "He must have had an iron nerve," one of them decided. Another, who knew him better, put it differently. "Harold," he said, "hadn't a nerve in his body."

The end of Gillam's story is a sobering one. He went only part way in his respect for science and in his use of it. When the Civil Aeronautics Administration began building modern airways in Alaska, just before the last war, he waited four years before he applied for the training necessary to use them. Even after he had qualified as an instrument pilot, he lagged in his technique. A fierce individualist, he seemed to prefer his own way of doing things. More than once, charges were filed against him by C.A.A. inspectors for false approaches on the new radio beams.

In the words of another pilot: "He got to the point where he almost acted as if he were superhuman. He was just plain asking for it."

Shortly after war began, Gillam went to work for a construction company, hauling workers and supplies for emergency airfields. He abandoned his familiar Pilgrims for the company's twin-engine Lockheed Electra, and began flying back and forth between Alaska and the United States. For the first time, his friends began to worry about him. He often overloaded the plane, bucking as violent weather as ever and flying exhaustingly long hours.

"I'll bet," his old pilot, Oscar Winchell, sadly predicted, "the way he's goin', Harold won't live a year."

Winchell was wrong by a few weeks.

On the morning of January 5, 1943, Gillam left Seattle for Alaska with a load of freight and five passengers. He had been warned that a storm was moving toward the Alaskan coast. Other north-bound flights had been cancelled for the day. After a sharp argument with airport clearance officers, he had taken off anyway.

So sure was he of his time-tested skill that he ignored air regulations en route. He did not make one position report over his radio all the way north.

Four hours out of Seattle, the plane entered dense fog. Gillam went on instruments. Still he kept radio silence. He proceeded blind until he was over the southeast tip of Alaska. Then he approached for landing at a new Army field on Annette Island, following what he believed to be the southeast leg of Annette's radio range. But the airways map which he carried was out of date. Annette's courses had been changed, and he was following the northeast leg.

Confused, he made a series of turns, trying to orient himself. The Electra was flying at 6,000 feet, rocked by strong winds, with heavy ice weighting the wings, when one of the engines stopped.

As his plane went out of control, falling toward earth under its load of ice, Gillam called out over his radio.

"I am in trouble!" ground operators heard him say. "One engine is out!" After this he was too busy to give his position, if he knew it.

The plane, according to an engineer who was aboard, hit a violent down-draft and dropped 4,000 feet "almost before we knew it. It was pitch dark and the fog was almost down to the ground, but now and then through a hole we could see peaks or trees flashing by.

"I yelled to the man beside me to fasten his seat belt. The plane swerved just in time to miss one mountain. Then we saw another looming straight ahead. There was an open spot near the top and Harold gunned the engine trying to make it. But our right wing hit a tree. I called out to the others. There was no answer. All I could hear was the hissing of the hot engine in the snow."

By miracle, no one was killed in the crash. The nose of the plane was buried in deep snow and the wing was snapped off.

The fuselage, dropping into a gully, was shattered by a falling tree, with the right engine smashed to pieces.

Several of the passengers were injured, however, and a girl aboard, a government stenographer, died after forty-eight hours. She was Gillam's first and last passenger fatality.

Gillam's condition was alarming. The cockpit had been crushed on top of him. He had a large gash in his head, and seemed stunned, dazed, quite unlike himself. He nonetheless went to work at once, tearing up aluminum for shovels, building snow shelters, cooking meals. He built signal fires and insisted on tending them himself. For five days, no help came. The food supply was already very low. On the sixth day Gillam took a few scant provisions, some matches, and a parachute for warmth, and left his passengers.

"I'm going up on a ridge," he tersely announced. "Maybe I can sight a definite landmark. If I do, I'll go to it."

He walked away alone into the steep, frozen forest. It was the last time that anyone saw him alive.

The starving survivors, some of whom finally stumbled down the mountain in desperation, were to wait a whole month, before they were finally rescued. The search for Gillam's plane was conducted under an almost impossible handicap. The plane lay only seven miles up the mountain from sea, only sixteen flying minutes from the Alaskan fishing town of Ketchikan. But as he had made no position reports during his flight he could have crashed, so far as search parties knew, anywhere on the long route from the United States to Alaska.

A query was sent to every telegraph station along the entire route. Coast Guard boats scouted deep into the bays and inlets. Forty planes, Army and bush, searched the coastal mountains.

But repeated snow and sleet storms, worst in half a century, beat down and the pilots, flying only by daylight, saw no sign of life in the jagged, heavily timbered country. It was believed that Gillam's ship had dropped into the ocean.

One wonders what had become of the dauntless tradition of northern rescue, which Gillam had honored so magnificently on behalf of Eielson. The reason is hard to find and the fact disturbing to many: the hunt, after only two weeks, was called off.

Two more weeks passed before the crew of a patrol boat, quite by chance, sighted two of the survivors running up and down, sobbing and shouting, on a lonely shore at the bottom of the mountain.

The other survivors were also rescued, and search was begun for Gillam. His frozen body, wrapped in a parachute, was found several days later, on a nearby shore. He had apparently died of his head injury, not long after leaving his passengers in a vain attempt to find help.

His flying boots hung on two sticks beside him, bottom up.

The government, after an investigation, decided that the tragic crash had been due to pilot error. Most of Gillam's fellow flyers prefer to judge it another way. "His engine quit him," they insist. "That could happen to any of us. If his engine hadn't quit him, he'd have made it again."

They do not like to discuss his final accident. But they will talk with awe, for hours on end, about the flights in which he foiled the elements—so boldly, so brilliantly, so usefully, for so long.

Chapter 8: **BOB REEVE**

Bird of the Glaciers

Bob Reeve's hair turned snow-white when he was thirty-eight years old. This is not surprising: he is the only pilot in Alaska who has made a practice of landing on glaciers. He is probably the world's only specialist at this frosty and risky line of work.

Reeve has a very different personality from most of the Far North's pilots. The others are men of few words, but he talks fast and suavely, wise-cracking all the time. He is fond of wearing fine clothes, after work hours, and owns a dozen custom-made hats. His interests are varied. Active in Republican politics, he ran for the office of Alaska's Delegate to the United States Congress in 1952.

He is a high-strung man, always in a hurry. "Let's vamoose!", he'll snap at a tardy passenger. "Okay, let's vamoose!" Until his doctor ordered him to quit, he was a heavy chain-smoker. More than once, he has seared his chest as a cigarette dropped inside his shirt during landing.

"I have spent more time flying sideways to see if my ship was on fire," he genially boasts, "than any other pilot in history!"

Reeve has flown more than 14,000 hours bush-style and made twenty-one forced landings. Until 1943, when he crashed in thick fog, he never damaged a plane beyond repair. His back was hurt in this accident, but up to that time the most serious injury he ever suffered as a pilot was when he dropped into a hayfield, climbed out of his plane—and was kicked in the face by a horse!

Sixteen of his forced landings were caused by failure of old models of the Wright Whirlwind engine.

"I was a guinea pig for those engines," he says. "I helped take out the bugs." Today, as he watches formations of Wright-powered bombers go roaring overhead, he proudly shakes his fist.

"There's part of old Reeve in every one of those damn things!" he boasts.

Bob Reeve and a twin brother Richard grew up at Waunakee, Wisconsin. The family is of old American stock; an ancestor settled on Long Island as early as 1690, and Reeve's great-great-grandfather served in a Connecticut regiment during the Revolutionary war. His grandfather, a lawyer, was one of the original settlers of Wisconsin's Sauk county.

Reeve's father, a telegrapher for the Chicago and Northwestern Railroad, chose Waunakee as his home because the University of Wisconsin was close by and he could easily send his boys to college there. But Bob, from an early age, showed signs of incurable wanderlust. When he was only fifteen years old, he ran away, faked his age and enlisted in the Army. He became an infantry sergeant in World War I. His father persuaded him to go back to high school, after the war was over, but one year of it was all he could take. He headed for the West Coast, this time, working at whatever odd jobs he could find, and roamed as far as China.

Once more his father persuaded him to come home and finish his education. Like Eielson, he began to study law. Then he broke away again and headed south. He worked in the business office of a newspaper, but felt stifled. "When I was just a boy," he says, "I resolved that I would never work at a desk indoors." Next he got a job working as handyman and "swamper" for a barnstorming pilot in Texas. The man taught him to fly in return for his services.

"Eating was awfully irregular," Reeve says. "We missed many meals to buy parts for the plane. But I was never happier. At last I was doing what I wanted to do."

In 1929 he went to South America and worked as one of the first pilots on Pan American-Grace Airways' pioneer mail run. He set a speed record between Santiago, Chile and Lima, Peru. He made the second night flight in history up the west coast of the continent, and in 1930 flew the mail 1,476 hours— a world record at the time.

For two years scorched pampas, dense jungles and tropical peaks slid beneath him as he pioneered these southern routes. "I returned to the States a well-to-do man," he says, grinning. "I'd earned the money like a horse. But I spent it like a jackass."

In 1932 he decided to head for Alaska.

"I'd seen every country to the south," he explains, "and I wanted to have a look at the north."

Alaska has held him ever since.

He stowed away in the chain-locker of a steamer, as he did

not even have enough money left for the journey, and arrived in the north, with two dollars in his pocket, in the spring of the year.

Stopping at Valdez, a small seaside town on the southeast coast, at the foot of towering snowcaps, he found a wrecked Eaglerock biplane and got a job repairing it for its owner. Then he rented it from the man, at ten dollars an hour. Neighbors helped him clear a cow pasture for an airfield and he was ready to fly.

His first customers were two grizzled prospectors. They wanted him to take them to a small island called Middleton, 150 miles offshore in the Gulf of Alaska, where they planned to stake claims. They admitted that they had been unable to find a boatman willing to take them out through the heavy seas to the storm-lashed isle. But they told him that they had once been to Middleton and seen a "big, long beach" there, ideal for airplane landings.

Reeve flew them over the tossing waves, in his wheeled, single-engine craft. The trip took two hours. When the bleak island was sighted he flew low, following the shores around, looking down on steep, boulder-strewn, surf-beaten banks.

"Where's your beach?" he shouted to his passengers.

They couldn't find it.

He decided that he would have to come down on the likeliest looking sandspit. It was not as likely as he judged. The ship nosed up in "fluffy, pea soup sand," a thousand feet from shore. The propeller was too bent for take-off.

He straightened the prop blades with a wrench and started the engine, but the plane would not budge. The men pushed and pulled; they could not dislodge it from the soft surface. Then Reeve noticed that the tide was rising; and fast.

Only a piece of remarkable luck saved the plane. Wading to shore, he stumbled across an old block and tackle, washed in from a shipwreck, banging against the rocks. He and his passengers buried one end deep in the sand, tied the other to the Eaglerock's wheel axles, pushed planks under the wheels and pulled the plane slowly through the surf to land.

They dragged it a whole mile overland before they found a stretch of land firm and long enough for Reeve's take-off.

He got the plane into the air, but as he headed back toward Valdez he flew into a lashing hail-storm. With the engine at full power, he could hardly keep the ship aloft. It was a long, harrowing journey through the driving sky and over the crashing breakers, and when he reached Valdez landing was impossible. The town was completely hidden; only the tops of cloud-wreathed mountains told where it must be.

His fuel was running very low.

He decided to make a try for the port of Seward, one hour away, the only other town nearby that had a small landing field.

He made it. Only five minutes' gas was left in the tank when he set the Eaglerock down.

"Then and there," he says, of his first flight in the Far North, "I started sharpening my wits, a process which has continued ever since."

In the years that followed, his reactions became lightning-swift, his judgments sharp as edged steel. His daring rivalled Harold Gillam's. But his contest was not so much against stormy sky as against treacherous terrain. Reeve, who became known as "the glacier pilot," made his reputation on snow and ice.

He began this work in 1933. Only once before had landing been made on one of the North's lofty rivers of ice. When Joe Crosson and S. E. Robbins had come down on a frozen slope of Mt. McKinley the previous year, it had been with such risk and damage to the aircraft that the company for which they worked refused to allow further trips. Glacier-flying was hardly a trade that the hardiest airman would enter by choice. Even Gillam shunned it. Reeve did not try it as a stunt. There was a practical reason.

The town of Valdez, when he arrived there, was as poor as he was. The story was much the same as that of Fairbanks, with nearby gold mines worked out. Everybody knew that there were promising gold deposits in this coastal region, but they lay high above the town on the steep, glaciered slopes of the Chugach mountain range. On the tipsy boardwalks of the ghost town, in dingy pool halls and shabby cabins, men talked of the wealth that was so near and yet so costly and difficult to reach with mine equipment. Everybody said there was a fortune up there. Everybody wanted to take a chance on it.

Reeve, who by this time had another plane, a Fairchild 71, was willing to take the chance that would make mining possible on the lofty range.

"I had to eat to fly," he says. "Also—I had to fly to eat!"

He agreed to take a prospector named Jack Cook to a claim called Big Four, six thousand feet high, on the slope of Brevier Glacier. The trip was to be an experiment. Cook promised that if he could land him on the glacier he would give him a contract to haul up all the supplies needed to turn the claim into a working mine.

It took only twenty minutes to lift Jack Cook to the claim that he had reached before by days of difficult climbing. But the trial trip was not encouraging. As Reeve sums it up: "The first time I landed on a glacier I flew into the side of a mountain."

"There's the place!" Cook yelled, as the ski-equipped Fairchild hovered over the huge slope of a snowcap. It took a knowing eye to find Cook's site; only a tiny dot of ore pile marked the claim.

Reeve flew to the bottom of the glacier, banked and started climbing. But the snowy rise, with no horizon for perspective, "plumb fooled" him. What looked like a three percent grade was more than fifteen percent. His plane began to stall. He could not turn. Towering mountain walls had him locked in on both sides. "I was flying," he says, "straight into a booby trap!"

He cut the engine, and his ship ploughed smack into the deep snow at the top of the grade. Luckily, the depth of the drifts saved both men from injury. They worked all day digging the plane out and shoveling the start of a runway—"sort of a shelf"—for take-off.

The take-off was dramatic. As Reeve revved up the engine, he and Cook looked ahead down a sheer 6,000 foot drop to the ocean glimmering far below. Like a car on a mammoth shoot-the-chutes, the Fairchild roared down the steep slope—and dropped into the sky.

Reeve made another trip to the Big Four the very next day.

"I couldn't back out," he says. "I told them I could do it."
This time he was careful to fly in at a steep climb, landing on
the bottom of the glacial slope. Hitting the snow at a speed of
eighty miles an hour, the plane moved less than 400 feet before
it stopped.

In just one week, Reeve succeeded in flying eighteen tons of
equipment to the Big Four in his small Fairchild; a mill, a
crusher, tables, a compressor, oil, coal, pipe and building mate-
rials for houses. The mill shell weighed a thousand pounds, and
there was hardly an inch to spare as he hoisted it with a jack
through the plane door. Later he delivered a load of Diesel
engines, wrapping the heaviest parts in mattresses and dropping them by parachute.

Clarence Poy, the manager of the new mine, was delighted.
It would have taken many weeks, he said, to haul these supplies
up to the Big Four with horses, and the cost to the company
would have been too high: at least 35 cents a pound. Reeve
had delivered it all in one week for only four cents a pound.

He began flying to other mine sites as well. There was a
clamor for his services. Late in the spring, when snow melted
at sea level, everyone thought that he would have to give up his
glacier trips till the next fall. But he solved the difficulty by
using mudflats as a runway at Valdez, taking his ski-plane off
from their slippery surface at low tide.

Tourists from the United States stared with amusement at his
600-foot mudflat "runway." Grass and daisies clustered in the
muck, and a red flag was planted at the end to warn of a ditch
and a mountain stream.

The tourists laughed at a sign painted on his small shed
hangar: ALWAYS USE REEVE AIRWAYS. SLOW UNRELIABLE UNFAIR

AND CROOKED. UNLICENSED AND NUTS. REEVE AIRWAYS—THE BEST.
He hadn't written it, but he liked it.

They laughed, too, when they saw Reeve driving to work in shabby clothes in a Model T Ford marked AIRWAYS OFFICIALS. And they laughed at his plane, which he bolstered against the tide at night by hoisting the tail onto empty oil drums. The battered Fairchild was held together with baling wire, and the floor was patched with grocery boxes, labels still on.

But they didn't laugh when they learned what Reeve was doing in the Valdez country. His prestige grew with the years. He earned enough to buy several more second-hand planes, and he opened up many more mines; the Mayfield, the Rough and Tough, the Little Giant, the Little Rose and a dozen or so others. The population of Valdez doubled. The ghost town came back to life.

Only by trial and error did Reeve master his unique trade. It took much nerve and will to learn it. There is, he says, something almost unearthly about landing on glaciers. Perspective is confusing and the glare of the sun on the crystallized snow is often blinding. Even on a cloudy day, the glare is so bewildering that it is risky to fly at an altitude lower than 1,000 feet.

Dropping down to land, he says, is "like sticking your head in an enamel pail." Each landing is like a forced one. "Judging where the snow is," he explains, "that's the first thing. You might level off 500 feet too high and come tumbling down in a stall, or you might approach too low and smack into the drifts."

As he learned on his first glacier trip, it is almost impossible to judge the angle of the surface below. Steep slopes appear as flat. Once he landed on an icy grade and had just cut the engine when his plane began sliding backward toward a precipice. He got the engine started again just in time to regain control. After that experience he always landed with his foot poised to kick the rudder and skid the plane, if necessary, at right angles to the incline.

In the weird light, the depth of the snow is also almost impossible to judge. One day a prospector riding in the cabin of Reeve's plane got the scare of his life. Suddenly he heard the engine stop. Then, to his horror, he saw Reeve open the cockpit door and swing his foot out. He thought his pilot had lost his mind.

"Don't leave me! Don't jump!" he shouted, grabbing Reeve's shoulder.

Reeve, who was half way out the door by this time, stared at the prospector as if it were he who had lost his mind. "What's the matter?" he snapped. "We're there. Those are the Black Mountains, and there is your claim."

The terrified prospector turned to look out the window. Snow pressed against the panes. He realized only then that the plane was not in the air, but had landed, gently sinking deep into drifts so soft he hadn't felt the impact.

Reeve himself could not always tell when his plane met the earth, when the snow was deep like this. He set up rows of black or orange flags, ten at a time, beside the claims for his return trips. "When I saw all ten," he says, "I knew I was approaching. When I saw only one I knew I must be on the ground."

But once, landing in a new place, he was marooned eight days in deep drifts. The shovel that he always carried in his plane was not enough to clear a runway. Take-off was impossible; the plane was sunk as in a bed of feathers. He sat helpless in the cockpit, day after day, on the mountain, till at last a strong wind blew up and swept away the drifts.

Deep snow, however, was the least of his worries. The huge, ponderously grinding glaciers of the Chugach Range are among the most treacherous places on the face of the earth. Much of their surface, rough as broken glass, is covered with icy pinnacles and with "unitaks" (jagged crags of rock) which sometimes tower as high as a thousand feet. Ridges of bouldered moraine crisscross the frozen mass, and it is cut throughout by yawning crevasses, some, as Reeve puts it, "large enough to hold cathedrals." The snow often forms a deceptive thin cover or roof over such death-traps.

Once Reeve flew straight into the boulders of a snow-hidden moraine. The impact deflected his plane upward 200 feet, cracking the landing-gear tubing. One summer, when sun melted the drifts over one of his glacier runways, he discovered to his horror that he had been landing repeatedly on the snow roof of a yawning crevasse twenty feet wide and hundreds of feet deep!

Dozens of corpses lie in the dark chasms of the Chugach glaciers. One night Reeve nearly joined them.

He was eating a late supper in the town cafe, that winter evening, when two haggard men stumbled in and asked him whether he could take off at once for Valdez Glacier. "Martin's up there!" they stammered, terror in their eyes. Their story was a grave one. They and their companion George Martin had been crossing the glacier on foot toward a mine when a sudden, blinding storm had blown up. It was twenty below zero, and as they'd huddled in the snow Martin had frozen his feet. When the storm had abated, he'd found that he couldn't walk a single step. They'd had to leave him. Unless he were rescued at once, this very night, he would die.

Dusk was already deep outside the restaurant windows. Reeve knew that Valdez is the most dangerous of all the Chugach Range glaciers, so jagged a mass of crevasses and ice pinnacles that he had never tried to land on it, even by daylight. But he hurried to the plane with the two men and took off at once.

Arriving over the glacier, he could not see well enough in the gloom to chance landing on its snow-covered surface. Taking a long gamble on boulders, he chose to bring his plane down on one of the dark streaks that he knew to be moraines. The rough impact with the earth was a lucky one.

As fast as they could, he and his passengers snow-shoed to the gulch where Martin lay. It was too late. They found him dead.

By this time it was pitch dark. As Reeve was feeling his way back across the glacier toward the plane, he stepped over the edge of a deep crevasse.

He grasped a ledge as he fell, and just managed to hold on, hanging above the abyss in the dark, till his companions arrived and pulled him up. The experience so shocked him that he has never since been able to walk with ease in the dark, even on a level sidewalk.

This accident on foot was the most serious one that he ever had in thousands of flights to the glaciers.

"Part bird," Alaskans say of him, as they said of Gillam. Other pilots, as in the case of Gillam, were baffled by his uncanny skill and frankly curious about his technique.

"Just plain drudgery," Reeve comments, rather shortly, when

asked how he did it. Taxying across the surface of a glacier he would stop every thousand feet, he says, lean out of the cockpit and carefully study the terrain ahead. Coming down to land, he would circle repeatedly, tediously, studying the surface below. How was he warned of crevasses that were hidden under thin snow roofs? "Just a kind of dim outline of a depression," he says. "Maybe the way the sun shone on the snow, a little glazed look to the surface, a little deeper shade than the rest."

He says that he memorized the tortured faces of glaciers in summertime, when the snow was gone from the lower slopes. He noticed that the safest places to taxi would be along the edge of moraines, where the crevasses were usually narrower and shallower than elsewhere.

He set up flags to mark safe runways near the claims, or he would circle overhead till prospectors had outlined a landing strip with lamp black in the snow. Landing in new places, he found that it was useful to throw out gunny sacks to help him judge his altitude as he came down.

He learned these tricks, and many more. But it was a good share of luck as well as skill that made his glacier record possible. "Fantastic luck!" he himself says.

Winds could never be predicted, and, as Gillam had learned, air spills through the passes of Alaska's southeast mountain ranges, in winter and in summer, like steep, sudden waterfalls. During one of his take-offs his plane was smacked back to earth five times before he got it airborne.

Another time, as he came down to land on a mountain top, one of the violent gusts of the region, known to Alaskans as "williwaws," lifted his Fairchild like a leaf and hurled it over the edge of a sheer, 5,000-foot drop.

He opened the engine full throttle and fought for control, but the plane went from a fall into a semi-flat spin with skis, wing tips and tail surfaces striking snow benches all the way down.

The next thing he knew, he insists, he was leveled out, flying through a canyon at an altitude of only 200 feet.

"In those twenty seconds," he says, "I figure I should have run out of luck 100 years in advance!"

On another flight he was heading through twisting, windswept Keystone Pass, dodging fog and fighting strong updrafts that repeatedly "sucked" him "into the soup." The fog got so thick that he was forced down. He spiraled onto a small, snowcovered bar in the middle of a river.

Then it happened. With deafening thunder, "the whole side of a big, white peak broke loose." A mammoth avalanche, "thousands and thousands of tons of snow and ice," crashed down the canyon wall, damming the stream and blocking a road, but missing him. Men who witnessed the avalanche believe that it was caused by the vibration of his engine. He likes to think so.

"Not every pilot!," he boasts, "has set off a major snowslide!"

The most daring of all Reeve's glacier flights was made in 1937, serving a mountain-climbing expedition of the New England Museum of Natural History.

The party, headed by the famous mountaineer Brad Washburn, wanted to scale Mt. Lucania, a peak in the Canadian Yukon, some 240 miles from Valdez. Lucania was at the time the highest unscaled peak in North America. Many men had talked of climbing it, but none had tried. The biggest obstacle was not the mountain itself, but the fact that it stood in the middle of the vast, desolate St. Elias "ice cap," one of the largest glacier systems in the world. It would be a staggering task for a party with supplies to reach the base of Lucania overland.

Washburn, who had heard of Reeve's work, wrote him a letter from Boston, asking whether he would be willing to fly the expedition and its supplies out from Valdez and land them on Walsh Glacier, at the foot of the peak.

Reeve knew that it would be a long trip for his small Fairchild, over "the meanest kind of wilds." Beyond this, landing would be a dangerous experiment, for Walsh is a lofty glacier, 8,500 feet above sea level, far higher than any of the glaciers back of Valdez. He knew that specially equipped light planes had operated from slopes this high in the Swiss Alps, but to the best of his knowledge no ski-plane with a load of freight had ever landed and taken off at such an altitude.

Unable to resist the challenge, he promptly wrote back to Boston, agreeing to service Washburn's expedition in his single-engine plane—at his usual charter rate.

Early in May he flew the bulk of the expedition's supplies to the glacier, hauling them first to snow landing at a part-way refueling point, the Kennecott Mine, and ferrying them on from there. He was glad to find that his Wright engine, operating with a leaned fuel mixture, performed as well at Walsh Glacier as it did at sea level. As it turned out, it was not altitude that was his greatest peril. Rather, it was the change of seasons.

He had planned to make all the flights under winter conditions, but Washburn was delayed and did not arrive at Valdez until early June. By this time the snow was melting on all but the loftiest mountain slopes. Walsh Glacier, both high and well sheltered, would doubtless still be safe for ski-landing, but the midway refueling stop would no longer be possible. In fact, there would be no place on the 240-mile route where the plane could land until it reached its destination.

Washburn was anxious. "Can you make it?" he asked.

"I can try it," Reeve told him. "Anywhere you'll ride, I'll fly."

On the morning of June 21 Reeve and his passengers wading in mud at the Valdez flats, loaded 350 pounds of extra gas and equipment into the cabin of the Fairchild. Reeve removed the plane door so the freight could be thrown overboard in case of trouble. Without this freight, Washburn's expedition could not climb the mountain. With it, the plane could carry just enough gas in the cabin for the return trip. Fuel in the tank was barely enough to reach Lucania.

The heavily weighted ship sloshed up from the muck, heading northeast. Soon it was bucking a thirty-mile headwind. Everybody knew what this meant. The fuel margin would be still closer.

In two hours, Reeve had flown half the distance to Lucania. The weather was more and more threatening. Low fog wreathed the ice fields. Scattered squalls swirled among the peaks. Sheets of moisture, traveling sideways, warned of turbulence.

"Should we turn back?" Washburn asked.

It was a good question, for if Walsh Glacier should be fogged in, the gas would be almost gone, and forced landing would have to be made somewhere else, if possible, in the midst of the desolate "ice cap."

Reeve told Washburn that he was willing to continue.

"You know," he explains, smiling, "if you turn back that first time you're liable to find yourself doing it over and over again."

Dark rain clouds bore down and down as the Fairchild flew on. The wind grew gustier. In another hour and a half the plane was approaching the foot of Walsh Glacier.

Washburn has never forgotten what happened next. As he tells it: "Flying into that valley was like entering a tunnel with a dead end. A mile on either side of us almost vertical cliffs of ice and rock rose into the clouds. Below us tossed the rough surface of our glacier. Seven or eight miles ahead the valley floor and walls melted into a murky ceiling, the lower surfaces of which we were just skimming. Behind us the storm was dropping down.

"He used the black 'slits' of open crevasses to come in safely. He throttled back the motor and dropped steeply to a point in the middle of the cracks. With the stabilizer slightly tailheavy and the motor idle, we dropped at a fast rate. About fifty feet above the crevasses Bob gave the motor full throttle and pulled sharply back on the stick. He cleared all the cracks but the last little ones; the tails of the skis touched these, and we settled down to a perfect three-point landing in the snow a dozen yards beyond." *

In this "perfect" landing, however, the skis dropped deeply. The Fairchild sank up to its belly in hidden cracks.

This high glacier, far from coastal moisture, had fooled Reeve. Here there was less dampness, less settling and packing, than on the glaciers close to Valdez. Snow conditions had

* *Sportsman Pilot*, January, 1938.

changed since his earlier freighting trips here, a fact which he had not been able to recognize from the air, and "dry, fluffy, white stuff like hoarfrost" had formed a more misleading cover over the glacier surface than any that he had encountered elsewhere.

It took two hours to dig the Fairchild out, shovel a channel, and move the plane to a firmer spot. Reeve shook hands with the mountaineers, wished them luck and climbed aboard for take-off. Revving the engine to full power, he waved and the plane started ahead.

It wallowed only twenty feet—and dropped deep into another crevasse.

By this time snow was beginning to fall.

The men pitched tents. As the snowfall was now too heavy for take-off, Reeve climbed inside with the others. They prepared a meal, and decided to take a nap.

Several hours later he awoke to a maddening sound, a sound that he could scarcely believe. It was no longer snow that was beating down on the tent. It was heavy, drenching rain!

Spring had come to the glacier, and now it was unlikely that an airplane take-off could be made from its thawing surface until the next winter!

The storm lasted four days. Gradually, the snowy surface of the glacier was turning to slush. Reeve became more and more impatient. Three times, he got the mountaineers to help him dig the plane out and drag it to firmer ice ridges from which take-off might still be made. Three times, he failed to get the Fairchild into the air.

His predicament looked more and more hopeless. The temperature rose to 58 degrees above zero and the glacial ice became so rotten that the men, stepping carefully, broke through the surface as they walked.

At last, on the fifth night, the rain storm stopped, and the temperature dropped abruptly to freezing level. By morning a slick, two-inch crust had formed on the glacier. Reeve rose early and stood in front of the tent, gazing out over the immense sea of glittering ice, debating what to do.

Washburn says that he will always remember the sight of his troubled pilot, silhouetted against the rising sun, soberly figuring his chances. The ice before the plane was thin. The slope was extremely short. A ten-mile downwind would make take-off still more dangerous, toward the chasms that yawned below.

"You can leave the plane here," Washburn suggested, "and walk out."

There were two ways of hiking to civilization. By skirting canyons and fording swollen rivers, Reeve might reach Kennecott Mine, 150 miles away. Or by inching up and down the precipices of a 16,000-foot snowcap, he might make his way to a tiny Canadian settlement called Burwash Landing, some 60 miles away.

Reeve had little time in which to make his decision. Minute by minute, the rising sun was thawing his fragile runway. He turned to Washburn, smiling.

"I'm no mountain-climber!" he told him. "I'm a pilot. You can skin your skunk—and I'll skin mine!"

Now he was all impatience. He asked the mountaineers to help him empty the plane of everything he might need in case of forced landing on the way home: tools, emergency supplies, food. They objected that this in itself could be a death warrant.

He told him that there was no other way; not one pound of extra weight could be carried if he were to have any chance at all of getting the Fairchild off the mountain and into the air.

He carefully loosened the blades of the propeller, flattening each one for utmost power. His helpers were meanwhile doing their best to brush frost from the wings and fuselage.

He said his farewells, climbed aboard, and the roar of the engine broke the silence of the glacier country. The plane began to move ahead.

"I got up pretty good speed," Reeve remembers, "till I hit a crevassed part. Then I went right through again, but I pulled her out—I wasn't stopping—that was an awful strong plane, and I figured sooner or later I'd get it in the air. It ran about ten thousand feet—bang, bang, bang, like a surfboard—there wasn't enough lift, and I was getting no place fast. Ahead I could see big open crevasses two to twenty feet wide. Just to the left was a smooth icefall and a five-hundred-foot drop-off.

"I made a sharp turn and dove right over it toward the valley wall. The drop-off gave the ship just enough forward speed. It missed a huge crack and sailed into the air! That was the greatest feeling in my life bar none!"

Washburn and his party later reached the summit of Lucania, and were heralded throughout the world for this history-making climb. Little was said of the gambling pilot who had made it possible. Washburn, who has worked with many pilots in Switzerland, Canada and Alaska, says: "Bob Reeve is without question the finest ski pilot and rough-country flyer I have seen anywhere."

For exploits like this, Reeve earned a reputation of being a man without fear. This was not the case. Once, riding as an airline passenger on a trip in the United States, he got off before he reached his destination because he did not like the way the captain up front was handling the plane in a snowstorm. Reeve has often felt uneasy on the airlines of the United States. But he continued down the years, confident at the controls of his own small plane, setting records for daring in the Far North.

He left Valdez in 1941 and continued his "one-horse" freighting operation, first out of Fairbanks, then out of Anchorage. The Army and the Civil Aeronautics Administration, when they arrived, found him a hard case. He did not seem to appreciate the new airports and airways that were built to make flight safer and easier. "All you need to be a pilot in Alaska today," he irritably complained, "is a duckbill cap, a briefcase, a watch with seven hands on it, a slide rule and 300 hours in the air—100 dual, 100 solo and 100 padded!"

Required by law to install a radio in his plane, he refused for many months to learn how to use it. "What do I want with a radio?" he told inspectors. "I have enough troubles of my own without a gadget like that!" The C.A.A., in a period of three months, grounded and reprimanded him for at least a dozen offenses against air safety rules. He also ignored wartime approach procedures at the new military airports.

One evening, landing at the capital town of Juneau without giving the customary notice, he caused an air-raid alarm. "What's the matter?" an officer shouted. "We nearly shot you down!" Reeve shrugged his shoulders, highly annoyed. Another evening, almost out of fuel, he landed at Fairbanks during a practice black-out. "Who gave you permission to come down?" an irate warden demanded.

"Come down?" he snapped. "What am I supposed to do, hang up there like a balloon?"

But Reeve could be forgiven many things. He did a superb freighting job for the Army. During the war period he hauled a total of more than 1,000 soldiers, more than 1600 tons of military freight, in his small, battered planes.

The man who had been the only bush pilot to land on glaciers now earned another distinction. He was the first bush pilot to fly regularly out the fog-and-wind-swept Aleutian Island chain.

Military and airline pilots who have flown the Aleutian route can testify that Reeve's trips to the region were as dangerous as his glacier flights; perhaps even more dangerous. It is well-known that Aleutian weather is just about the worst in the world. Fog and storm roll ceaselessly across the bleak rock isles; ceaselessly and violently. Hundred-mile squalls windmill the props of bombers, scatter piles of lumber, send heavy oil drums whirring through the air, tear off tin roofs. Few of the Army's aircraft losses in this theater during the war were directly caused by the Japanese. Most of the planes crashed in foul weather, before airways could be installed.

Reeve signed a contract with the Signal Corps to fly key men and rush equipment into the Aleutian area, and he made more than 200 trips "to the westward," most of them in his Fairchild 71.

He caused a sensation among the troops at new Army bases. His small red plane, parked on one of the airdromes beside a row of Liberators and Mitchells, looked like a child that had toddled into a line of troops. The Fairchild was not even as big as the gas trucks that rumbled up to refuel it! Time and again winds tore it loose from its heavy oil-drum moorings. Ground crews chuckled as they telephoned Reeve late at night in his Quonset hut quarters: "Sorry, your ship got away again." Army pilots in the quarters would laugh as he angrily slammed down the receiver: "Damn it, there goes Leaping Lena again!"

They would swap stories about Reeve as if he were something out of Ripley. How could he do it? His Fairchild had no de-icing equipment, in this humid region where icing was a constant threat. His engine was an old Wasp that he'd used in South America as long ago as 1929! His plane cruised at only 110 miles an hour, landed at only fifty-five, in the violent winds.

"He scares hell out of us," one dispatcher said. "We've given him up for lost many times. But somehow he always makes it down."

Reeve did it, of course, by means of the same canny "contact" techniques that all of Alaska's bush pilots used. The gamble was consistently greater, that was all. "I'm still sharpening my wits," he gaily wisecracked. "I have to keep sharpening my wits."

One stormy day flight control men picked up an emergency call. "This is Seven Zero Three Four. Will you give me a report on the day's tide? I say again, I want the tide, the *tide*—how high is today's tide?"

"What's that guy flying?," a new soldier asked. "A plane or a boat?"

"A plane," the others told him, and added, as if to explain everything: "That's Bob Reeve."

Bad weather had forced Reeve down on a seaside mudflat. The ocean was rising, lapping and licking toward his small ship. As it happened, the day's tide was to be the highest of the year. Advised of this, he splashed off the mudflat at once, climbed "on top," circled until he found a hole in the fog, spiraled down through it and fought his way just above the earth to the nearest field.

Despite his skill, Reeve had a serious accident, in 1943, near the base at Cold Bay. Fog forced him "on top" and he learned over his radio that all airfields within the short range of his plane were "socked in" to the ground. Darkness fell and his fuel ran out. He started down blind for an emergency landing. Only a glimpse of phosphorescent breakers, sighted at the last moment, enabled him to make a controlled landing on a strip of beach. His back was hurt, and some of his passengers were also injured. They were all rescued by the Army, but his plane was demolished by wind and sea.

He was sobered by this accident. He was also sobered when his twin brother Richard, an Air Force Captain, crashed to death in Illinois. But he continued his work with bravado until the war's end, and after the war he built his "one-horse" outfit into one of the most important airlines of Alaska.

Reeve Aleutian Airways has pioneered the first scheduled service in history to the islands of the storm-swept chain. It also flies out over the open sea to the Pribilof fur-seal islands, nearly 300 miles to the north. Reeve has built it into a large organization, covering 3,400 miles of far-flung routes and doing a million dollars worth of business a year.

The ancient red Fairchild has bowed out to a fleet of three DC-3s, three large amphibian planes and six smaller aircraft. Fifteen younger pilots now work under the famous bush veteran's command. Chief pilot is Bill Borland, son of the mechanic who crashed to death with Eielson in 1928.

In 1950, at the age of 53, Bob Reeve decided to stop flying, and he has since spent his time managing his airline from the ground.

"I realized," he explains, grinning philosophically, "that I had not only run out of my own luck, and all my friends' luck, but about a thousand other people's luck as well!"

Chapter 9: ARCHIE FERGUSON

The Flying Clown

Not all the Far North's pioneers were skillful ones. In a land where airplanes were more important than automobiles many old-timers, trappers, miners and others, decided that they too wanted to fly.

"Land and take off," one said, "nothing to it! A man can do anything in Alaska."

The stories of some of these men are hard to believe, but reliable witnesses confirm that they are true.

There was Tom Roust, a rough-and-tough carpenter at Nome. He was in his fifties when he bought a wrecked Standard and repaired it. "I can handle her," he told his friends. "I know wood." He got his plane off the ground, sashayed over town and crashed, breaking two ribs. Then he repaired the ship and flew many times.

Eskimos would dive into their huts when they saw him in the

air. Mothers would call their children in from the streets. "LOOK OUT! There goes Tom!" But he never had another accident.

There was Joe Scoric, a high-strung little Russian who had paddled over from Siberia in a skinboat, shortly after the Revolution. He, too, was middle-aged when he decided to get a plane. "I wish I have a wing," he said, "so I can jump over da big hill!" Scoric took flying lessons, but they did him little good. Puzzled, he tells about how he lost his plane, trying to land on a beach.

"Well I got too much air speed, gotta get 'em slower. I glide down. I keep looking. I got 'em sixty. I got 'em fifty. Now I got 'em forty. Then I got no air speed! Then I got no airplane! Wind tips tail, swings it in da ocean, I got to swim to shore!"

There was Henry Kroll, the "Mad Trapper," at the town of Seldovia. Kroll was a heavy-set fellow, a trapper and prospector who had once worked as a one-man band in a circus. He got a plane so he could hunt and spot quartz outcroppings from the air. He took one flying lesson, but was so wild and stubborn that the instructor refused to give him any more.

The "Mad Trapper" was a mad flyer. He'd come in low over town, idle the engine, play a banjo and sing and yell to people in the streets below. But he was a capable flyer. An inspector later gave him a license, and he logged 500 hours in the air before a windstorm wrecked his plane.

None of these "old-timer pilots" could compare with Archie Ferguson. A prospector and trapper who had lived in Alaska since he was a boy, Ferguson not only became a pilot, but did much more. Basing at the Eskimo village of Kotzebue, beside the Arctic Ocean, he pioneered the farthest north flying service under the American flag.

Gnarled and dumpy, with fat cheeks and friendly eyes, Ferguson looks like one of the Seven Dwarfs. He has an intense zest for life, a boundless sense of fun. His laugh is high and rasping, and he shakes with mirth till the tears roll down his cheeks. "Archie loves a lot of things," Alaskans say, "but nothing so much as laughter." His nervous energy is inexhaustible. He does not talk, but cackles like Donald Duck. He does not walk, but half-runs, half-hobbles wherever he is going. "He will fly three hundred miles," a friend once said, "ask three hundred questions, answer them all himself and fly three hundred miles back."

Ferguson lives in a green wooden house at Kotzebue, in the midst of tumbledown Eskimo turf-topped huts. "All built with six-by-six timbers from our own sawmill," he says proudly. "This darn place is strong." His large living-room looks a little like an aeronautical museum, but an odd one. Clippings and pictures of airplane wrecks line the walls, and there is a broken propeller nailed over every door.

He laughs, as a visitor stares at them. "They say I got more crack-ups than any pilot in Alaska," he amiably explains. "But I ain't killed anybody yet. Oh gosh, I wouldn't do that!"

He no longer flies actively, but in his heyday he could think of nothing else. No civilian pilot in Alaska, government records show, has put in longer hours aloft than Archie Ferguson. One summer month he logged a total of 185. (Airline pilots in the States are not allowed to fly more than 85.) Even on stormy days, when it was impossible for him to make a trip, he had a habit of climbing into his plane and buzzing dizzily round and round above the village. "Gosh," he said. "I dunno, somehow in a plane I feel differ'nt. I'd go nuts if I couldn't fly!"

"FERGUSON AIRWAYS," he proudly advertised. "ANYWHERE, ANYTIME." The name was splashed in huge, white letters on the side of his red wooden hangar. He not only flew himself, but hired a staff of other pilots and owned a fleet of several small planes, Cessnas, Stinsons and a Waco. He sold more than $50,000 worth of air transportation a year, serving settlements hundreds of miles from the nearest standard road or railroad.

Ferguson did an important war job, freighting for strategic mineral surveys, airport construction and mapping projects. The "Little Man," as he is affectionately nicknamed, became a big name at the top of the continent. But he went about his useful work and flight in the prankish manner of a clown.

A tame trip was irksome to him. An incurable practical joker, he liked to frighten passengers by switching off the gas for a moment in mid-air. He especially liked to frighten school teachers newly arrived from the states. "We're comin' ta the Arctic Circle!" he would shout. "Ya can't see it but ya'll sure know when we hit it. The engine'll quit! There's no air in that darn circle for eight hundred feet!"

More than one teacher screamed as he cut the motor. He never tired of this trick. "Oh boy, I'd oughta teach school myself!" he would say, shaking with laughter. "At least I got more learnin' than that!"

He captained his Cessna with a kind of frantic enthusiasm, shouting so loud over his radio that operators at airways ground stations would have to tune down their receivers to save their eardrums. Time and again, during the war, he was asked to lower his voice, to make his reports formal and brief. He did not seem to understand. Sometimes he would stop shouting and sing or whistle.

"Nome Radio, Nome Radio," he yelled one day during the war. "This is Cessen Two Zero Seven Six Six. Gosh, it's startin' ta rain up here! Looks like some awful dirty stuff ahead! Gimme yer weather in the clear!"

The ground operator reminded him that Alaskan wartime weather information must, except in cases of extreme emergency, be broadcast in code. "Cessna Two Zero Seven Six Six," he asked, "do you declare this an emergency?"

"Yer darn right!" Ferguson barked. "Yer darn right it's an emergency! Any time I'm in the air it's an emergency!"

It really happened. The late General Simon Bolivar Buckner, who was in command of the Army in Alaska, declared that Ferguson was the greatest comic character he had ever met. "Maybe he's a pilot," airline captains said, "but he shouldn't be." Someone called him the craziest pilot in the world. "But crazy like a fox," Alaskans warn. "You have to know Archie."

Ferguson, with his parents and a brother named Warren, arrived in Alaska in 1917. "Times was bum," he explains, "and Papa read some story so we hit north." They traveled from Nome far into the Arctic wilderness, prospecting for gold. Ferguson loved this life. He seems to have had a remarkably happy boyhood.

"I used to run a nozzle at a mine," he says. "Gee, I liked that!" The family traveled hundreds of miles by dog team, and he enjoyed this, too. "Gosh, the snow got deep, and we had nice, great big dogs!" When he was old enough, he hauled freight up the Kobuk River in a home-made scow. "I'd hardly never sleep. Drunk coffee ta stay awake. It's a long, long ways up the Kobuk in a boat, yer darn right. I sure liked ta run the river!" He trapped, too, in the Colville region. "I sure liked that. Really went ta work and caught a lot o' foxes. Hardly a year I wasn't the high man."

In 1919 Ferguson married Hadley Wood, the grand-daughter of the chief of the Kobuk Eskimos. His brother also took an Eskimo wife. Even before they entered aviation, the Fergusons were outstanding pioneers in this northerly part of Alaska. They built a sawmill and several trading posts. They opened a mink farm. They started the first movie house north of the Arctic Circle. They brought the first automobile, an International "pickup," to the Arctic coast, and rode it up and down on the winter ice between villages. They also imported the first cow and the first motorcycle.

Ferguson says he got the idea of flying from the motorcycle. He mounted it on skis, he explains, and would hurtle over the frozen sea at a speed of forty-five miles an hour. "Hadley 'n' I'd put on our nice parkys 'n' ride between towns. It was a great big police model, a Harley. Gosh, we had a lot o' fun with that thing!" One sub-zero day he stopped short just in time before an open crack four feet wide. He built a snow ramp on the ice beside it and froze the snow. He tied a log to the motorcycle, in case it dropped through. Then he told his wife to stand beside the crack so he could "line himself up," drove away, and roared back toward her with the engine wide open.

"I hopped right over," he says, still excited by the memory, " 'n' lit ten foot on the other side o' the crack. Gosh, I was really flyin' then!"

He had his first plane ride in 1926, with Noel Wien, and was badly frightened. "Wien looped me 'n' I purty near fell out. Gosh, I was so scared I couldn't get my hands loose from the sides of the plane!" From this time on, however, he was obsessed by aviation.

Visitors to Kotzebue say that he would keep them awake half the night talking about planes. In 1931 he decided to become a pilot. He sent to the United States for a Great Lakes trainer, paying four thousand dollars for it, and another thousand to have it shipped north by boat. He also hired a pilot whose name he found in a magazine ad, Chet Browne of Colorado, to come to Kotzebue and teach him how to fly.

Browne gave Ferguson a total of sixty hours of instruction, more than seven times as much as the average student needs. He wanted to give him still more, but Ferguson's impatience won out. "Gosh," he complained, getting angrier and angrier, "ain't ya never gonna solo me?"

On the great day Browne, who seems to have caught some of Ferguson's prankish spirit, hid an alarm clock under the plane's seat and set it to ring in ten minutes. "Go right up over town," he told Ferguson. "Climb to a thousand feet and circle around, and be sure you take your time."

Ferguson took off smoothly enough and circled steadily, till the alarm went off. His plane banked crazily and went into a steep dive as he forgot the controls and fumbled under the seat to try to locate the noise. "Gosh I was scairt," he remembers, laughing wildly. "I thought it was some kind of a signal!" He managed to get the plane back under control, but was so disturbed that he landed on a sand bar instead of coming back to the home-made strip that was his airfield.

Ferguson's shrewd, soft-spoken Eskimo wife was not enthusiastic about her husband's flying. His first trip with a passenger was hardly one to reassure her. He flew from Kotzebue to a settlement called Shungnak, 175 miles up the Kobuk River—and made an atrocious landing. As he himself tells it: "That passenger must 'a' had on four suits o' underwear 'n' three suits o' pants. I could hardly stuff him in the cockpit. I come down ta land at Shungnak on a smooth place in the river but gosh I missed it 'n' hit on the next bend. If he hadn't 'a' had so many clothes on I'd 'a' killed him fer sure."

Ferguson's parents, then living at Shungnak, were always terrified when they heard the sound of his engine in the sky. He scolded them bitterly after one of his first crack-ups there. "I couldn't tell the wind," he explains, " 'n' I told Mother when I came back to be sure 'n' put up a sock or make some smoke fer me. Next time I went over 'n' buzzed the place 'n' she made that fire darn quick! I landed fine! I went in the house 'n' Papa was askin' her 'where's my new pants?' They couldn't find 'em nowhere. 'Oh dear,' she told Papa, 'I musta used 'em ta make Archie's smoke with!' Gosh she was scairt, she'd burned up his nice new pants. Poor Papa!"

The Fergusons went into the aviation business in a big way, despite all Archie's mishaps. He and his brother bought more planes and some expensive radio equipment. More pilots were hired to instruct him and fly the ships. "I've been trained by experts," he cheerfully boasted, when he had been flying for nearly fifteen years. "I've had an awful lot o' instructors, but I still need a lot more."

A surprising number of Alaska's younger pilots have, at one time or another, worked for Archie. "The Ferguson College of Technical Knowledge," they called his operation. He paid well. But few men stayed with him very long. One reason for this was his strictness. He neither smokes nor drinks, and has always frowned on such habits in others. Always an early riser, he expected the same of his pilots, and would rouse them from their beds long before it was light enough to fly. An insatiably hard worker, he was never satisfied with their efforts, and it drove him to distraction when one of his pilots was weather-bound away from Kotzebue. "I suppose yer boozin' or heaven knows what yer doin'," he would shout over the radio. "The weather's fine here! Come on back!"

He was enraged if one of the pilots had trouble taking off from Kotzebue's snowy runway in winter. Whatever the depth of the drifts, he would stand beside the field jumping up and down, nervously hitching up his pants, shouting and swearing. "Gosh, hurry up! Oh, hurry up! Golly, I guess I'll have ta do all the flyin' myself!"

His pilots did not care to travel with him. One day during the war a man named Harry Swanton, who had just arrived from the United States, was hauling Ferguson toward Nome through rolling fog. Treetops flashed past the windows. "Okay," Ferguson told him, "ya got an instrument rating, fly her on instruments!" Swanton tried to do so but could not orient himself on the Nome radio range. "Yer headin' right back ta Kotzebue!" Ferguson screeched, as he recognized a mountain through a hole in the mists. "What's the matter with ya? Can't ya fly?"

Swanton mutely pointed to the compass, which showed the plane to be headed toward Nome.

"Oh that darn thing," said Ferguson, "it don't work. I took a screwdriver 'n' give it a coupla twists but it ain't good for *nawthin'*. Gosh, let's git out o' here!"

Ferguson had a strong dislike for scientific air navigation. "I can foller a dog trail awful dirty," he said, "but the beam, it's sure hard to figger out." He preferred to "run a plane" by trial and error. A government inspector once advised him to study meteorology. "Metrinology?" he snarled. "What the devil is that?" He did not even maintain any of the usual pilot records. "I never keep no logbook," he said. "Just when I crack up, that's all."

One winter day his ship, heavily loaded with freight, approached Shungnak. By this time there was a small radio station there, and it warned him that the river ice was only three and a half inches thick and unsafe to land on. This did not discourage him; he had managed to land there before on only three inches. He came down, "sassy-like," his passenger said, "singing a tune." The plane broke through the ice. Several inches were sheared off one blade of the wooden propeller.

Ferguson took an ax and chopped off the other side to match. "I'll fix this baby!" he told the nervous passenger. "We're really goin' ta fly today!"

The plane ran three miles down the river, rattling like a sawmill, before it was airborne.

Ferguson is particularly proud of this flight. "Gosh," he says, "I rolled the stabilizer way ahead 'n' used the belly-flaps 'n' the little devil went right up in the air with me. She flew me practically like a stall, till I got her up ta eighty, 'n' then she stayed that way. I guess it just happened ta be right!"

As he gabbled over the radio, telling about his difficulty, ground operators were horrified. "NC-18799 heard on 02042," flashed one airways emergency despatch. "Says broke propeller, now en route to Kotzebue."

He landed safely. C.A.A. inspectors who later examined the

stubby prop could hardly believe that it had kept a plane in the air. They suggested that it should be put in a museum.

"An airplane will do what ya make it," Ferguson always insisted.

He proved this masterful idea to himself, and also made aviation history, one day at the town of Kiana. He had parked his Cessna the evening before on a short river bar. In the morning he discovered that the water had risen during the night, swirling to the belly of the ship. "Think of that!" he says, still indignant. "My whole darn runway was gone!"

He stood a moment, brooding. Then he snapped his fingers. "Okay," he told a crowd of watching Eskimos, "I'll take her away by boat!"

Several of the dusky women helped him drag the Cessna over to the bank and haul it up onto a barge. They blocked the wheels and tail. Some of the women climbed aboard for the ride. He mounted into the cockpit, opened the engine, and the barge roared up the river by aircraft power to the nearest field.

"Talk about power!" he bragged. "You'd oughta seen that thing walk up the river! Ten miles an hour, she made upstream. I'd cut her close and let the wings clear the banks. The engine, she never got hot—I run her at 1200 'n' she stayed at 375 Farnite. I went round them bends so fast the natives thought the Japs was coming! That rig looked like a big bulldog! I never seen an airplane done better than that!"

Ferguson was one of the first pilots in Alaska to use a plane for wolf-hunting. He first tried this challenging sport with one of his pilots, Maurice King, in 1935. As King flew the plane the "Little Man" pointed a shotgun out the window toward a large wolf and fired. He didn't hit the wolf, but he did hit the propeller. The plane crashed. He was still enthusiastic however. Altogether, he claims, he has killed sixteen wolves from the air—"'n' cracked up every time."

There is no story that Ferguson likes to tell better than the story of the swearing parrot. Other pilots like to tell it, too. "It could only happen to Archie," they all agree.

"I just sent to the States fer a bird to keep us company," he says. "Gosh, a bunch o' sailors on the boat learned him ta swear 'n' by the time I picked him up at Fairbanks he knew every cussword in the English language. I put him in a cartoon box in the end of the plane 'n' took off with one o' my pilots, Maurice King, fer home. Gosh, we run inta the roughest air o' my life. Maurice was flyin' 'n' fightin' the plane 'n' I was fightin' the parrot. Oh gosh that bird was screamin', callin' me names sumpin' awful!

"We kep' him three years, till my big lead-dog killed him 'n' ate him up. He was purty, that bird, green—ya know how they're green? But he didn't like me—I really figger he thought I tried ta kill him that day on the trip. He'd scream 'n' dive fer me—no question, he didn't like me at all.

"But ya know, that darn bird—in the end he saved my life!"

It happened in 1941, when Ferguson, flying in foggy weather, was forced off one of his usual Arctic routes. Cruising among blurred hills, he thought he was approaching the village of Hughes.

"I'll be in in ten minutes," he shouted to Hughes radio operator. "Put the coffee pot on!"

"Okay, Archie," the operator answered. "Where are you?"

"Never mind where I am!" he yelled. He was less and less sure, himself. "Put the coffee pot on!"

Some ten minutes later he crashed in the winter wilds at least a hundred miles from Hughes. The plane was dragging under a load of ice. He opened the engine full throttle, heading for the nearest clearing, but one of the wings hit a tree.

"Then she quit flyin'," he says, cheerfully. "She was in a half-turn 'n' she hit flat. Gosh, that's a nice way ta put an airplane in! It sure is hell on the airplane, though!"

The wing was sheared, the engine torn out. Ferguson was knocked unconscious. His two passengers, a restaurant man and a doctor, mistook oil spattered in the cockpit for blood. They thought their pilot was dead. He revived just in time to hear them say so.

"Gosh, I really thought I was killed," he says. "I was afraid ta open my eyes, death was so nice, so quiet! Then I come to, reached up ta shut off the switch, and saw it was disconnected. My darn arm was broke, and there we was; radio tore out, motor tore out, not much grub, twenty below zero 'n' a hundred miles from anywhere."

The plane was down in one of the remotest parts of Alaska; "mountains all over, all low timber, no lakes or nawthin' there, and there wasn't even no rabbits, the snow was so deep." Ferguson had hardly been prepared for emergency. There was only one sleeping bag in the plane, only one pair of snowshoes, no gun, and little food. Most serious, because of his misleading call to Hughes, search parties would have only a false clue of where he was.

He was cheerful, as usual. He began building snow houses

and chopping trees. "Gosh, fellers," he told his passengers, as soon as the fog had cleared, "we're in too deep here. We can't get over the divide. Best thing ta do is git a bear 'n' kill it with an ax."

He started scouting, and soon found a ring of iced bushes which marked the "breather" of a bear hole.

"Come on," he told his nervous passengers. He gave the snowshoes to one, the ax to another, and bade them follow him as he wallowed back to it through the deep drifts. He had them help clear away the brush "so them bears kin come right out ta battle." Then he rammed a long stick deep into the hole and started stirring.

"Gosh, I kin feel 'em!" he shouted.

"More than one?" the men asked, edging away.

"Oh gosh, yes, I can feel sometimes one, sometimes two. Now I kin see 'em. I kin see their pink eyes shinin' in the dark! Oh, golly, here they come!"

The men turned and ran floundering toward the plane. Ferguson, stranded without a weapon, hurried after them. He was indignant. They were more so.

"You've got us in enough trouble, Archie," they told him. "You're not going to get us in any more."

It was Ferguson's frontier knowledge, however, that finally brought rescue. And this, strange to say, is how the swearing parrot happened to come to his aid.

"The only way out," he told his passengers, "is the radio." Slowly but ingeniously, he retraced the wires of the receiver. The battery, which he had found in a snowdrift, was dead; but he remembered from his boating days that a dead battery may be revived by heating it in a stove—"at least ya can git out a half-hour more." He heated this one beside the bonfire, and started shouting.

A voice answered from Fairbanks, more than 300 miles away. "Archie, we hear you. Planes are out searching for you. What is your position?"

He tried to answer, but the battery went dead.

For four days and nights more, the hungry men waited. There was no sign of a search plane overhead. They began to despair. On the fifth day, Ferguson made another try with the battery. "If you let her lay a while," he said, "she may work again." He heated it and made one more call for help.

"Tell Maurice King," he screeched, "that I'm right where we had all that trouble with the parrot!"

The call was heard. Operators relayed the odd message to Pilot King, who remembered instantly the flight that he had made with Ferguson and the profane bird two years before. He flew into the Arctic and located the wreck without delay.

Ferguson was determined to save his plane. Although it was more than 200 miles from Kotzebue, he hired a gang of Eskimos with sixty dogs to drag it back. The Eskimos had to cut their way slowly through many miles of virgin timber. When they reached the site, they found the plane covered with new snow. It took two days to dig it out. Altogether the unlikely expedition cost Ferguson $1,000.

"Sixty dogpower on it," he proudly wrote the C.A.A. inspectors. "Boys sure done a fine job getting it out. I am tearing her completely down and she will be as good as ever again. I hit awful hard as the big round stand on the smith greb skies, I put a one-turn twist in them. . . . I wish you people could see this ship. Motor is not hurt at all. . . . I got one spar four foot from end and I got all new parts from factory.

"Both skie boards snapped off rite at bottom of smith greb stand, the boards could not keep up with the ship HA-HA. I sure know how to handle them in a crack-up HA-HA. My arm is getting along fine, only thing there is a bend in it. . . . Now I see a man has to have a real wreck to have any sence and when I see ice on my wings now I don't have to be told what to do and when I see a tree I go around it, HA-HA."

The C.A.A., as might be expected, had more trouble with Ferguson than any of Alaska's bush pilots. This was not only because he disliked air regulations, not only because of his frequent accidents. Now and then, typing rapidly with two fingers, he would sit down and write a letter of protest about the new airways that were being installed. In one of these classic documents he complained about "a very dangerous obstruction" near Fairbanks.

"It is a bunch of radio towers," he angrily wrote. "It seems the C.A.A. are not happy unless they can stick up a bunch of towers on the sides to the fields and on the approach to the fields. . . . The one in Fairbanks I believe is most dangerous of them all . . . built rite side of a good road that shows up in bad weather and pilots are sure to follow this road in bad weather if they get caught. . . .

"Fairbanks weather was not so bad but heavy rainy swalls and was following the Chena Slough and all at once this nice road showed up. I at once got on the road and was doing fine till I saw this tower go by and I won't try to tell you how far I missed it but it was so close they nearly had no tower. . . .

"Kotzebue had a pretty nice field till the C.A.A. moved in

but now it is surroned by towers, wires, etc., and it is quite a trick to get into it without losing a wing. I think the only way we are going to be able to operate a plane in Alaska if the C.A.A. keeps on improving is to have underground airways. . . ."

He was also bitter against Alaska's new Army airports. "I went inta Galena," he says of one large base. "Some soldier told me ta call him on the down wind leg o' the beam. I said where the devil is that at? Oh, gosh, I musta been right on it. I landed okay but it took me an hour ta git out of that place. They told me I gotta git the weather. I told 'em I don't need no weather, it's gonna get dark, let me out o' here. They tell me every bend in the river, what clouds ta fly between, look out fer a certain plane, oh golly! Then they give me a little piece 'o' paper 'n' tell me ta give it ta the clearance officer.

"I must 'a' asked ten men—nobody knew where the devil he was at. I seen a guy diggin' a ditch and I says ta him 'Will ya take this piece 'o' paper so I kin git out o' here?' He says sure 'n' puts it in his pocket. I take off but gosh when I git in ta Fairbanks they jump me 'n' ask me why I left Galena without a clearance. I tell 'em I give it ta some guy, he was the only guy who would take it. Oh gosh, if I ever have ta go back there I'm gonna land on a sand bar, you bet!"

He was badly hurt during the war when he flew his Cessna into ice in a snowstorm. The ship crashed violently and a thirty-six-pound battery missed him by inches as it hurtled out the windshield. "I sure scattered that plane," he says ruefully. "All that was left was one ski 'n' the fuselage." His back was fractured, he bit a piece out of his tongue, and he was so frightened that he refused to board a rescue plane. He made a slow, rough journey home by dog team.

He was soon in the air again, however, and flew for many years more, plaguing and amusing inspectors over and over again. "Ya hear that noise?" he called in one day to the Nome station. "Gosh, that ain't static; that's a bear. Yeah, I gotta bear in the plane with me, jest a cub, I bought him ta train as a pet, but he's broke loose. He's climbin' right up here beside me, growlin' 'n' showin' his teeth—big sharp teeth! Oh gosh, he's tryin' ta eat up the fuselage! There's two of us up here now, but it looks like purty soon there's only gonna be one 'n' it ain't gonna be me! Stand by, I'll call ya every other minute!"

Narrow escapes were so routine with Ferguson that no one was surprised when he reached his destination safely. Alaska laughed about this episode for weeks. Rumor spread that the bear had been at the controls when the plane landed. "The best landing," someone wisecracked, "Archie Ferguson ever made."

It was like a comic short run off at double speed. Till Ferguson quit flying, in 1949, the show never stopped. But his air career deserves more than laughter. For all his antics, the Little Man did valuable work, risking his neck in bad weather over some of the Far North's loneliest wilds. His airline was extremely important to the scattered settlements that it served. And the fact remains that none of his countless crack-ups ever took the life of a passenger.

"The main thing in flyin'," he once said, looking unusually serious, "is airplanes are jest material 'n' ya kin rebuild 'em. Pilots and passengers hafta be born."

Chapter 10: **FRED MOLLER**
The Little Giant

Fred Moller was a flight mechanic for Pan American Airways in Alaska. He worked out of Fairbanks, riding the company's airliners and servicing them at way stops. His fierce devotion to duty on this job is a legend. Joe Crosson once said that Moller was probably the best flight mechanic in the world.

That is not all there is to Moller's story. Once, before he went to work for Pan American, he had been a pilot. He had made history. In 1928, he had been the first man in Alaska to use an airplane for prospecting. He'd wrecked the plane. The truth was that Moller wasn't much good as a pilot. But never, until the day of his death, did he give up the dream of flying on his own again.

"You can't talk long about Alaskan aviation," Crosson said, "without speaking of Little Freddie. He was more than a flight mechanic, more than a pilot. He was an institution."

Fred Moller was a proud little fellow. He stood only five feet high. He was wiry, skinny, spry as a rooster. Pan American listed him on the load manifest at 135 pounds. Everybody knew he was not that heavy, but nobody knew how much he really weighed. Sensitive, he refused to stand on the scales, and kept himself bundled in a lot of clothes. "Two or three suits of pants," said another mechanic, "and two or three sweaters and coveralls made a pretty big man of him."

Nobody knew how old he was, either. For ten years before his death in 1944 he had been telling people that he was fifty-two. Some said he was in his sixties. Others said he must be in his seventies. Others insisted that he was already getting bald when he arrived in Alaska, in 1901. Wrinkled and weather-beaten, he nonetheless had the energy and enthusiasm of some-one very young.

Nobody could quite figure out his accent. He had a rough speech, like a foreigner's. He said he had been born near Lon-don, England, but he had spent most of his life in the gold camps and towns of Alaska. He may have spoken a mixture of cockney and siwash. In summer he wore a British cap on his head, in winter a fur hood.

He was so shy, so earnest, so busy and so proud of his work in aviation that everyone liked to kid him. "Little Freddie," people called him, smiling when they saw him. "Saw Little Freddie over in the Co-op, just flew in from Nome. . . . There's Little Freddie, hopping down the street. . . . Say, what's your hurry, Freddie?"

Yet everybody, even Pan American's senior pilots, stood in awe of him.

Most people called him Little Freddie, but he also had other nicknames. Some Alaskans called him Shorty. A few spoke of him as The Midget. One of his friends called him The Little Giant. The Little Giant—that was the best name for Fred Moller, for his spirit was as large as his body was small. No one who knew him will ever forget him.

Moller and his father migrated to Alaska from England very early, during the Gold Rush. They lived a while at Nome, where he peddled papers and kindling while his father panned the beach. Once his father hit it rich, and the two of them went back to England on a pleasure trip. They returned to Alaska penniless. Soon after this his father went to the United States and disappeared. Freddie sent many letters trying to find him. There was never a reply.

He prospected a while, wandering all alone far into the Arctic, pitching his own camps, following the creeks to many new places. He seldom had any luck, so he got a construction job on the Alaska Railroad. He helped build one of the longest single-span bridges in the world, near the town of Nenana.

He was a "jolly good little worker" on that job, railroad old-timers remember, dependable even in winter when the wind blew up to forty miles an hour and the temperature dropped to sixty below zero. He knew every rivet on the bridge, and liked to speak of himself as a "steel man." He was so tireless, so meticulous, that one of the construction bosses offered him a higher-paying job in South America. He turned it down.

More than anything else, he wanted to go back into the Arctic hills and look for gold. He liked the long suspense of hunting colors and the rare excitement of finding pay dirt. He was sure that he would hit it rich some time. And he liked to live and work in the wilderness, all alone.

"Why, it's the only country!" he once explained. "The sheep are so tame the little fellows walk right up to you, and the young birds fly to your camp for crumbs. I had a pet fish, one place, a bull-head. That fellow was always around at meal-time for me to throw him scraps. You know, out in the hills there's no such thing as being lonely!"

He learned more about Arctic minerals than most men in the north. He became a friend of Dr. Alfred Brooks, then the United States government's chief geologist in Alaska. Brooks told him long ago what geologists confirm, more than ever, today; that the Alaskan Arctic, still almost empty of humans, holds untold riches—coal, oil, asbestos, nickel, lead, silver, tin, tungsten—even amber and jade. Moller knew that the most inaccessible parts of the Far North are full of promise. That is why he wanted to fly.

To a man of his experience, the aviation idea came naturally. He had tramped, "mushed" and floated thousands of slow miles. He had built his own automatic dams for sluicing, his own cabins, his own boats.

"You know," he said, "out in the hills we build everything and find a way to do everything. As I grew older I thought, by gosh, some means of transport must be invented to get over this country in the quickest way possible."

In 1923, when Ben Eielson landed at Nenana after his first flight in Alaska, Moller was waiting in the front of the crowd. He helped tie down the Jenny. Then he cornered Eielson.

"I told him I wanted something like that for prospecting," Moller recalled. "I asked him if he thought I could be a pilot, too. He really encouraged me."

The Little Giant made a trip to the States and took flying

lessons from the famous Spokane pilot Nick Mamer. The instruction ended badly. On one of his first solo flights Moller's plane crashed into a line of electric light wires. He was "in bandages" after that accident, he said, for a year and a half.

Returning north without money, he decided to train himself to be a mechanic. "First thing, I had to learn about motors. I'd go to the dumps and dig them out, them old motors to cut wood with woodsaws. I'd fix they up and get they running. After a while people found out that I knew all about it, and when they needed a man they'd send for me."

Next, like many another man on the frontier, he trained himself to be an aircraft mechanic. ("There are a hundred volunteers of the Mechanician Class in our town," the Fairbanks newspaper boasted in 1925, "who can assemble an airship in less than no time.") Moller soon became one of the best, servicing "machines" for men like Eielson, Wien and Crosson. He helped outfit the Wilkins expeditions. "I shoed their skis with the proper metal," he proudly remembered. "They had put wooden skis on. I told them they were liable to stick, and recommended they use some tin."

The more time he spent around the fields, however, the more he hankered to fly himself. He begged the pilots to let him borrow their planes. They usually refused. When he had saved enough money he bought one of his own. "I rustled around till I found a Waco cracked up that would be for sale. I bought her and we fixed her up."

He took more flying lessons, a great many more. He needed fifty-four hours of them, before his instructor would let him solo. Several pilots tried to help him. Noel Wien smiles when he remembers how hard the Little Giant worked at the controls and how much trouble he had. Fairbanks airfield old-timers all smile when they remember how hard he worked repairing his second-hand plane and the two damaged Curtiss OX-5 engines that he bought to go with it. Evening after evening, he could be seen at the field, intently welding the struts, covering the wings, puttering over the parts of two engines to make one.

He painted the ship bright green and polished it, "rubbing and rubbing to make her shine bright." On the Fourth of July, 1928, he strung small American flags all over the wings and fuselage. He even built a small model of the plane, perfect in every detail. And he gave his craft a name, like a boat: Anna. Some people think that it was named for an Indian sweetheart. Others say that it was named for his English mother. Moller would never say.

"The Anna," as he solemnly spoke of his Waco, made real history. Old newspapers confirm the fact that Moller, in the summer of 1928, was the first prospector in Alaska to fly his own plane. As the ship had room for one passenger, he decided to go a step further and launch his own small airline. He ran an ad in the Fairbanks paper:

BEFORE YOU TRAVEL IN THE AIR
SEE FAIRBANKS AIR EXPRESS

THE ONLY FAIRBANKS COMPANY GIVING
RATES TO PROSPECTORS AND MINERS

HOT SANDWICHES AND COFFEE
SERVED DURING FLIGHTS

WARM FLYING CLOTHES FURNISHED

He made the sandwiches himself, in his shack, and "always had a few extra parkys around" to keep his passengers warm. He always carried a pick and shovel and a gold pan in the cabin of his airliner, ready to work wherever he landed. He was not interested in hauling ordinary passengers, but he rode dozens of miners out to their claims on the chance that they would find the gold to pay him back. He would make a fifty-fifty deal with a prospector any time.

For nearly two years, he flew "the Anna" through the inland mining country. But his airline was not a success. Many of his passengers returned from the hills broke. Others met disaster, and he'd have to fly out to their rescue. "Their dogs would come back to a village, so we'd know the boys were in trouble, lost, drownded or killed by a bear, and I'd go out and hunt." He found one of his customers on a mountainside, "stiff as a board." Another had been eaten by a grizzly; "not much left of him but a leg and one shoepac." Trouble was an everyday matter on the airline. If Moller's passengers were not in difficulty, he was.

Experience with flying did not seem to help him. He could not learn to handle a plane. He was so small that he had to perch on a pile of cushions to see out, and he was high-strung and excitable in the air, passengers remember; "just like a jumping jack." Most important, those who knew him best say that his eyesight was poorer than he would ever admit, even to himself. In those early days, there were no air inspectors to check it. Although he managed to log a total of 500 hours in the air, he had nothing but disappointments as a pilot.

He had far more than his normal share of crack-ups. Much of his time was spent on the ground repairing the plane.

"Always busy mending a busted stabilizer or rudder," a friend remembers, "or a hole in a wing, or a splintered ski." His sad landings were a common joke. People began calling him the "Slap-her-down Kid."

One day mechanics at the Fairbanks field heard the sound of an engine and looked up to see who was arriving. "Hold your hats," said one, "here comes Freddie." The Waco dropped down in a sideways tilt, hit with a lurch, and flipped over on its back.

"What happened?" the Little Giant shouted, as he hung head down in the cockpit, silver dollars dropping out of his pockets.

"You just turned over," said a bystander, wounding his feelings so deeply that he would not speak to him for a week.

Once, landing at the town of Curry, Moller knocked several branches off a tree. He repaired the plane, climbed in—and slithered into another tree in take-off.

Another time, clad in a black-bear flying suit, he prepared for take-off from a snow-covered river bar near the Arctic town of Shungnak. He pushed the boulders to one side and set a row of small flags to line himself up. Then he climbed onto his pile of cushions.

"All fixed?" bystanders asked.

"Yup," he replied, raising himself and peering ahead.

"Can you see all right?"

"Fine."

He started the engine. Then, in the words of a witness, "by golly, he headed right for a pile of stones, smashed into it, and broke twelve inches off the end of the prop!"

Patiently, he picked the splinters up and fitted them together like a jig-saw puzzle. He slipped a piece of stovepipe on the blade to hold them in place, wrapped the whole with wire. Propelled by this classic piece of patchwork, he managed to take off safely, this time, and flew 300 miles home.

Moller usually carried an extra propeller in the plane with him. He also carried tools on all flights, and "a big butcher-knife and a saw to cut trees." They all came in handy. He couldn't learn to watch the winds. Nor, well as he knew the country, could he seem to recognize it when he was flying a plane. Again and again, he was blown off course.

Since "the Anna" carried only thirty-five gallons of gas, these confusions led to repeated long hikes. He was cheerful about this. Overland distance never seemed to dismay him.

Once, running out of fuel in the Koyukuk region, he came down on a river bar 200 miles from the nearest town. He built a raft of logs, floated downstream to the town, bought a canoe and some motorboat gas. Then he paddled laboriously all the way back upstream, fueled his plane and took off.

Nothing and no one could persuade the little prospector that he could not fly. Ben Eielson, whom Freddie called his "staunchest friend," was one of the few pilots who gave him any encouragement. Moller was always very proud of this fact. "Ben came right up to my hangar every time I came back from a trip," he remembered, "and told me 'Atta-boy! Keep going!'"

He kept going—until he lost his plane.

It happened in the spring of 1931. He left Fairbanks with a load of mail, heading for the town of the Eagle in the Forty-mile region. By the time his gas ran out he was circling confused in the Nabesna region, farther from his destination than when he took off. As he described it; "The motor pooped as I was crossing a rocky ridge. I saw a little pond ahead and just made the edge of it. CRASH! 'The Anna' was gone."

So completely was the plane demolished that he made a bonfire of it. Then, dutifully dragging the mail sack after him on a ski, he trudged several weeks overland, following a trail to the town of Big Delta.

Another pilot tried to rescue him. Learning his position from tiny hamlets through which he passed, the man flew low over the trail many times, searching. But Moller did not want to be rescued. He hid in the woods each time he heard the engine. "His feelings were hurt, that's all," Alaskans explain. "He just wanted to come in under his own power."

He did not have the money for another plane, so he built himself a twenty-six-foot poling boat and left Fairbanks by river to prospect in the Arctic. He was gone for two years. They were years of bad luck. He found little gold, and then, one day, floating down swift rapids in the Colville River, his boat tangled with low-hanging "sweepers" and capsized. His whole outfit sank to the bottom of the stream.

He swam to shore and hiked for many weeks across the tundra, living as best he could off fish, rabbits and berries. He hurt his foot, but made a cane of forked willow and hobbled on. When he arrived back in Fairbanks he was "thin as a sliver, pale as a ghost" his friends say. He was laid up six months with rheumatism.

He went back to work as a mechanic, this time for Pan American Airways, and helped build the airline's first Fairbanks hangar. It was not long before he had saved up the money to buy part interest in another plane. Pilots were appalled when they learned his choice; a Stearman biplane—at the time one of the fastest-landing aircraft on the field. "You'll get killed, Freddie," they warned him. "That's too hot for you." So many people told him this that he agreed to sell his interest.

He stayed with Pan American for the next ten years. If he was restless on this job, or frustrated, he gave no sign of it. Rising each morning at five, or earlier, he walked to work along the edge of the runway long before most mechanics were out of bed. He serviced Pan American's airliners as carefully as if they were his own. "If he was assigned to a plane," Joe Crosson said, "it was always the best." He figured out a new and better way of folding winter wing covers and insisted that other mechanics use it. He rubbed the cowling and waxed the wings as a housewife would polish silver. He snapped at others if their work displeased him. "A clean ship is a safe ship," he always said.

Promoted to flight mechanic, he worked a total of nearly 10,000 hours in the air aboard Pan American planes. Now and then, in the dual-control Electras of the day, pilots would let him have a feel of the controls. In the Pilgrims that were the workhorses of the run he had to ride behind in the cabin with the passengers. He wore headphones and heard the radio reports but his only way of communicating with the pilot was to shout or pass notes through a small opening between the cockpit and the cabin.

With time, he became as distinguished as a flight mechanic as he had been undistinguished as a pilot. He learned Pan American's routes by heart; their mountains, their rivers, their snow conditions and, equally important, their people. He knew all the Indian and Eskimo helpers at small way-stops by name. He was generous: at Christmas-time he never forgot a man, woman or child. He was also stern. He bossed them sharply as they flocked about the airliner to refuel or unload. He wouldn't tolerate a second's delay. "He'd do anything for them," Pan American pilots say, "and they'd do anything for him."

He bossed the pilots, too. He became such an expert on the route that the company assigned him the job of breaking in captains newly arrived from the United States and familiarizing them with the country. He herded them like sheep.

"You're just a kid at this game!" he told one, who had many years of experience on Pan American's southern routes, but none in the north. "You'd better listen to me!"

When another pilot insisted on heading off course, Moller poked a fishing rod through the opening leading to the cockpit and switched him on the neck. He threatened to spray still another with the fire extinguisher. There were several with whom he refused to fly. No captain, however high he stood in the company, escaped his sharp, exacting eye.

Title meant nothing to Moller. He had an ill-concealed scorn for desk workers and executives, especially those from New York who gave orders ill-suited to Alaska. "So you're the new traffic manager?" he asked one pompous arrival, and spat on the floor. When a group of visiting officials took a plane off Pan American's mail run to use for a bear-hunting trip, he followed them down the runway scolding them as severely as he would the Eskimos. "You can't do that!" he shouted. "Don't you know that this is an airline?"

For years he wore on his flight cap the gold band that is reserved, by Pan American regulations, for captains and first officers. No one wanted to tell him to take it off. "Or no one dared," said one captain, grinning. The truth was that the Little Giant had his own rank, and everyone knew how valuable he was to the organization.

In 1942, when a Pan American plane crashed in an icing blizzard on the Koyukuk Divide, Moller was the only passenger aboard. He took command at once. First he helped the pilot, a big, burly captain named Les McLennan, out of the wreckage. He told McLennan to help tramp a big OK in the snow for search planes to see. Then he started on foot through the wild country, leading the captain to the nearest settlement.

They had not traveled far when Moller discovered that McLennan had brought along the plane's Very-pistol as a souvenir. He was indignant. "Didn't I tell you not to pack anything you don't need?" he shouted. He grabbed it and hurled it over a cliff. When McLennan tried to chop a stump for firewood, and missed, he snatched away the ax and refused to return it. "Next thing you'll cut off your foot," he told him, "and then how will I get you home?"

Captain McLennan later reported that his flight mechanic bossed him severely all the way back to civilization. He could hardly complain, he added. Without the help of the canny little frontiersman, he was not at all sure that he would have survived.

In honor of Moller's tenth year of Pan American service the company staged a surprise party at the Fairbanks hangar. Joe Crosson flew all the way north from Seattle to attend it. Moller, who virtually worshipped Crosson, was pleased and "proud as a peacock," Pan American old-timers say. He prized the new two-starred service emblem on his lapel. It seemed to be the crowning moment of his career.

But it was not long after this that Moller announced, to the alarm and dismay of his friends and employers, that he was going to quit his job, buy a small plane, and fly once more on his own.

"I'm really a miner at heart," he told them. "A prospector. It's not the money, you know. But I got my old maps. I know where the tin and tungsten are."

He said that he planned to look for vital minerals for the government, minerals that were needed in the war.

In 1943 he paid $750 for a wrecked Curtiss Robin with a J-6-5 Wright engine. He moved from his cabin near the field to a tar-paper runway shack which also served as a nose-hangar for his plane. He worked in his spare time for many months, re-covering the fuselage and rebuilding the stabilizer. He painted his plane bright orange, this time, with a snappy black stripe. In November he announced that he had it ready to fly.

All his friends were deeply worried. He had not flown a plane for many years. He wasn't young. The boys at the hangar tactfully suggested that he let someone else give the ship its first test. He refused.

Everybody at the airfield was watching on the day when he climbed into the cockpit. Proud and excited, he revved up the engine. He waved happily to the crowd, as he taxied out. Then he began practicing S-turns—and smashed headlong into a Pan American tractor that was parked on the runway nearby. The engine of his plane was badly damaged.

He started all over again and worked many more months in his spare time, repairing it. When spring came he told his friends he had it ready.

"I'll be hanging in the motor in another week," he said, his eyes shining with expectation, "and then I'll go out and roam around."

He told Pan American that he wanted to leave his job as flight mechanic on the first of April. The company asked him to stay on a few days longer, as they were shorthanded that week. He agreed.

It was fair morning on the fifth of April when a Pan American Pilgrim, piloted by young Robert Bullis, a newcomer in Alaska, prepared to leave Fairbanks on the mail trip to Nome. Aboard, along with Moller, was his friend Ted Seltenreich, also a veteran mechanic, who was to take his place on the job. The hangar crowd kidded as they loaded the plane.

"Two mechanics," somebody said. "It's a sure sign of bad luck."

Moller went to the airport office to file the flight plan. He was in a chipper mood.

"Well, Pop," he gaily told the airport manager, "this is my last trip with the P.A.A.! From now on, I'll be flying on my own."

The next day, seven minutes after take-off from Nome on the return trip, the Pan American Pilgrim ploughed through the white haze into a snowy hill. All members of the crew and three Eskimo passengers were instantly killed.

The report spread fast throughout Alaska. In the airline shacks and along the runways, men were hardly able to talk about it. "Little Freddie was aboard. Little Freddie got it this time." Mechanics and pilots at fields all over the Far North stopped hammering, loading, checking, filing, couldn't find words to say.

Slow old-timers, prospectors and dog-mushers, stopped one another all up and down the Fairbanks streets. "Did you hear? Little Freddie was killed. Over to Nome." Some just stood. Others walked awkwardly away.

Nobody wanted to believe it. They hoped it might be a false rumor, till the newspaper hit the streets toward evening, and they saw his name in heavy black print.

The double funeral with which he and Ted Seltenreich were honored was one of the most crowded in Fairbanks history. Some of the roughest men in town wept openly as pilots and mechanics bore Moller's coffin down the aisle.

It is remarkable how often people still talk, warmly and with deep respect, of the Little Giant, the pioneer who could not learn to fly but served flight so well.

"He had the kind of spirit that don't die easy," one of his friends has said.

No man, in the history of Alaskan aviation, has been more beloved.

Chapter 11: **JACK JEFFORD**

Builder of the Airways

Pilot Jack Jefford, a big, raw-boned man with a keen, friendly face, is today top patrol pilot for the Civil Aeronautics Administration in the Far North.

He flies all over Alaska in an official plane with the winged, international-orange emblem of America's foremost civil aviation agency on the side. Flight-checking radio ranges, testing instrument landing systems, monitoring weather stations and hauling equipment, he keeps the new airways system running smoothly so that all pilots may use it safely.

Jefford is no ordinary airways inspector. Meeting him, you see at a glance that he was once a bush pilot. As he climbs down from his big government plane it's likely he's wearing an open fur parka over a pair of rumpled pants and sport shirt. His tie is askew, and a few locks of his unruly black hair are fallen across his forehead.

He'll stand there, easy-going, as if he were just the pilot of a battered Stinson, and his hand, almost automatically, will reach for a pocket. He'll start jingling coins. Pulling out one of the frontier's big silver dollars, he'll flip it onto his wrist.

"Odd man for a dollar?" he'll drawl, casually. "Just one time?"

No man, it is said, can meet Jack Jefford without matching a dollar with him. One usually leads to more. His easy manner and his good humor never change. Slow-talking, slow-moving, he goes about his official work as if it were some kind of a game. He is careless of dress, forgetful of time, and has, on the ground, an air of good-natured befuddlement.

But few pilots in America work as hard or captain their planes with such a range of skill. During the war one Army general in Alaska declared that he would rather fly with Jefford in a ship with one engine out through a blizzard than with most pilots on two engines through fair weather. This, the general explained, was not only because Jefford knows the north like a book and can "set a plane down on a dime." It was because he is a combination rare among airmen. An outstanding bush flyer, he is equally distinguished as an instrument pilot.

He has already logged over 15,000 hours aloft, more than most of the veteran pioneers. A younger man who did not arrive in the north until 1937, he has blazed a different trail from theirs. He has used his two-fold skill to help build the new airways. He, more than any other one man, has been the pioneer of instrument flight in Alaska.

Jefford grew up on a ranch in northern Nebraska. He was still a boy when he saw his first plane, a Curtiss "pusher," at a county fair. Fascinated, he spent long evenings afterward build-

ing airplane models, whittling the wheels and other parts painstakingly out by hand.

After he graduated from high school he got a summer job pouring cement for a contractor. "Backbreaking work," he says, smiling, "and on some of those hot, muggy summer days I'd see the transcontinental mail planes speeding overhead. Of course I felt that my calling was in aviation!"

He went to Denver, Colorado, got a job in a factory building machinery for jewelers, saved up the money for flying lessons and soloed at the age of nineteen. Then he "begged and borrowed" enough to buy a Curtiss Robin and started barnstorming with a brother, Bill. They opened a flying school at Broken Bow, Nebraska, but could find few paying pupils. The farmers of the region had had a series of crop failures, and people were still a little afraid of planes in that year.

It was in 1935 that Jefford did his first scientific work in the air, making high-altitude flights for the United States Weather Bureau, in Oklahoma. The hops, comparable to Gillam's, gave him his first experience in blind flying; they all had to be made at two o'clock in the morning, to an altitude of 17,500 feet. He spent much time practicing under the hood and qualified that year for a C.A.A. non-scheduled instrument rating, one of the first in the United States.

Returning to Nebraska after the weather contract expired, he managed the airport at Hastings a while. He barnstormed some more, stunted and joy-hopped. But this casual kind of flying no longer interested him. In 1937, when he had a telegram from a chance acquaintance, offering him a job in Alaska, he took the next boat north.

"I'd heard that aviation was important in Alaska," he explained. "People depended on it and respected it. It wasn't just a stunt business."

Like many another Far North air pioneer, Jefford arrived in Alaska with less than a dollar in his pocket. Hired by an outfit called the Hans Mirow Flying Service, he worked out of Nome bush-style for three years, and served as tough an apprenticeship as anyone. There were still no real airports or airways anywhere.

One winter day he was heading across a mountain range in a Gullwing Stinson, fighting violent wind, when his small plane was suddenly sucked down at the rate of 2,000 feet a minute. He couldn't get it back under control. The ship crashed against a snowy peak.

He was not hurt, but the left wing tip and landing gear of the Stinson were damaged. Worse still, a sixty-mile wind was rocking the plane, which was perched at the edge of a steep precipice. He had no means of tying it down, no snowshoes to cross the deep drifts surrounding him as far as he could see. He spent several days and nights trapped in the cockpit till the storm died down and another pilot flew over and rescued him.

Jefford did his share of confused flying above strange wilderness. "I have never been lost over Alaska," he says, grinning sheepishly. "At least I always knew I was within the borders of the Territory." He had his share of close calls. "She's a beautiful country," he exclaims, emphatically, "but she can be cruel!" He had not been long in the north, however, before his remarkable skill was noticed.

Another pilot was forced down that winter in the bleak Nulato country with a woman passenger and a sixteen-month old baby. Their supply of food and heating fuel was almost gone. Five flyers, searching by daylight, could find no sign of the wreck. Jefford decided to have a try by night. After cruising for a long time over the snow in the dark he sighted the lost party by the flash of its campfire. Night flying, at the time, was rare.

In another outstanding "mercy" flight, he hauled Frank Alba, a prospector with a broken leg, to Fairbanks through a night snowstorm. The blizzard was one that no pilot would have battled except in extreme emergency. He navigated "Gillam-style," flying very low above a river in the driving snow. The people at Fairbanks, accustomed as they were to rugged air work, reported that his landing there that night was one of the most sensational the town had ever known. The snowfall was so thick that Gillam's mechanic had to "talk" him down by radio.

The dour and proud Gillam, who seldom had a compliment to pay another pilot, was so impressed by Jefford's skill that night that he offered him a job flying for him any time he might want it.

Jefford had soon earned a place of prestige in the north's tough flying fraternity. The Eskimos were so admiring of the newcomer's ability to find his way over the Arctic regions, even in the dark, that they gave him a nickname: "Owl-Eyes."

His first flying for the government was done on a survey of the Far North's wandering reindeer herds. It was the first complete survey ever made. He flew a Reindeer Service official,

Charles Burdick, far and wide across the Arctic, following the ruffled animal tracks over the snow in all kinds of weather and setting him down in the wilderness wherever he could, as close as possible to the herds and corrals.

The tri-motor Stinson in which he did this work was larger and faster-landing than most of the planes that had operated on skis in this part of the country. He brought it down in one difficult spot after another, often through dusk and "milk bottle white" so confusing that he could hardly see the ground. Not once, during the entire expedition, did he damage the plane.

Once he flew Burdick to the Akolokotuk corral, for a meeting with a group of herders. Arriving over the corral, he saw that the snow around it was much too deep and soft for safe landing. Cruising above the area, the two men sighted a wind-swept lake, several miles away, where the drifts were not so high. Burdick suggested that they come down there and hike back.

"Well," said Jefford, mysteriously. "We'll see."

Burdick was surprised as he flew back to the corral. He started circling right over the enclosure, looking down at the snow within, which had been trampled down flat by the hoofs of the herd.

"Hell," he finally told Burdick. "I can set her down right inside!"

Burdick was not so sure. He was flabbergasted as Jefford neatly landed the tri-motor plane into an entrance little wider than the wing-spread, and managed to stop it just before it reached the other end of the short enclosure.

"One of the ruggedest flyers I've ever seen," Burdick says of Jefford, "and also one of the gayest."

One dark night as the two men landed at the coastal settlement of Unalakleet, a crowd of smiling Eskimos met the plane. Jefford greeted them like old friends, and they followed him eagerly from the air strip to the trading post.

"Have you got my fiddle?" Jefford asked Charlie Traeger, the old-time store-keeper. "We thought we would play a while."

A Laplander got his saxophone. Several Eskimos fetched accordions and guitars. Jefford started fiddling and was soon leading the crowd in a sentimental tune. The room was full of happy, dusky-faced people, and others crowded in the snow outside. The harmony was good, Burdick says, although Jefford was just a self-taught fiddler and the Eskimos were all playing by ear.

Jefford still keeps his fiddle at Unalakleet, and says that he would rather be grounded there by bad weather than anywhere else.

In the summer of 1939 he made a new kind of Alaskan air history. He was the first American pilot to guide a boat systematically, for any distance, through the ice pack; a technique which the Russians pioneered, in their sector of the Arctic, long before we did in ours.

The spring had been freakishly cold, and the ice pack heaviest in years. Nonetheless the steamer *Columbia,* first boat of the summer from Seattle to Nome, left the United States as usual in June. Her Captain hoped that by the time he reached Alaska's northwest coast the ice would have opened enough for him to make it through the rest of the way.

He figured wrong. Forty-eight miles off the mouth of the Yukon River, still about 150 miles to the south of Nome, he was forced to drop anchor. The sea ahead was choked with icebergs. The first mate, climbing the mast, reported that the great mass of floating chunks extended as far as he could see.

For four days and nights the *Columbia* stood motionless. Her Captain, a towering, bluff Norwegian named A. A. ("Big Andy") Anderson, had traveled this route for twenty-five years and never faced such a crisis. The steamer's food and water supply was running low. He sent an emergency message to Nome, asking if a bush pilot might be willing to fly out and scout the ocean beyond.

The safest plane for scouting out over the sea would have been one on floats. But there was no float ship at Nome at the time. Jefford offered to do the job in a single-engine Lockheed Vega. It did not even have a radio to communicate with the steamer, but he asked a local operator to rig up a home-made broadcasting set, and took off as soon as it was ready. It was ten in the evening. His brother Bill (who had followed him north from Nebraska) rode with him on the flight. Bill sat behind in the cabin with the radio.

They flew to the mouth of the Yukon River, struck out over the open sea, and tried to contact the *Columbia*. They could not. Their radio, they discovered, was not working. In Jefford's words it was "definitely a bunch of junk," scattered over the floor with the antennae trailing out the window. His brother, shouting through an aperture between cockpit and cabin, shook his head despairingly; he was unable to fix it.

Jack decided to have a try himself. As the Vega sped through the air, some 6,000 feet aloft, he leaned backward and pushed himself through the opening into the cabin, letting the plane "fly itself" until his brother could crawl up front. An able self-taught mechanic, he managed to get the radio in operation, and he and Bill exchanged places again.

They were navigating through the summer night entirely by dead reckoning. Jefford had marked the *Columbia's* position on a marine map, but it was no easy matter to find the steamer in the vast, mottled sweep of sea and ice. Calling the captain, Jefford asked that all her lights be turned on and that all possible smoke be made. After this it was not long before he sighted a twinkling, puffing speck below and flew to it.

Passengers waved and cheered as he dropped low over the steamer's decks and rocked the Vega's wings.

Then, heading northwest, he flew for five hours over the sea, scouting in vain for a break in the ice jam. He stayed in the air as long as his fuel allowed, and landed back at the Nome field with less than a half hour's gas in the tanks.

The next day he made another try. He managed this time, by throttling down his engine to less than fifty percent horse-power, to stretch his search time to seven hours. He also took along an experienced Coast Guard man, Kurt Springer, to help in the hunt. After much exploring they discovered a wide-open "lead" of water among the icebergs, large enough to let the steamer pass. This "lead" began some seven miles north of the *Columbia* and extended the rest of the way to Nome.

Carefully, they scouted and rescouted the seven choked miles that lay between the steamer and the open "lead." The task would not be easy, they agreed, but it looked as if the *Columbia*, guided by the plane, could, by following a crooked course through the channels and shoving her way against the smaller icebergs, reach the open water.

Jefford radioed this opinion to "Big Andy." Then began a process of navigation new in United States marine and aviation history. It was difficult; the *Columbia,* an old single-screw vessel, was not very maneuverable. It was dangerous, for she was no icebreaker. Her plate was only five-eighths of an inch thick. It was also very complicated. While Jefford's radio allowed voice broadcasting, the steamer was not equipped for this, and all of "Big Andy's" messages to the plane had to be tapped out in code.

Jefford made repeated low passes over the *Columbia,* heading each time in the direction he thought the steamer should take. He flew two miles in each pass, long enough for the nautical compass, lying on the floor of the plane cabin, to steady down for a reading. The Coast Guard man then shouted out the indicated heading, and Jefford relayed it over the air to the boat. He also gave the Captain frequent advice.

The ship's operator dispatched anxious queries in dots and dashes.

"How should we hit this one?" he would ask.

"Easy to the left," Jefford would reply.

"How much longer is this lead?"

"Half a mile."

They worked by this method for a while, but it was not satisfactory. The *Columbia* was moving as slow as she could, but even so she moved too fast for co-ordination with the "seeing eye" above. Jefford, making the two-mile passes and flying wide circles for his return approaches, was not able to advise "Big Andy" closely enough. The *Columbia,* during one of his departures, rammed into a large iceberg and sprang a leak. This was too much for the captain. He said that he could not risk his passengers' lives any further.

Jefford then hit on a new scheme. Circling closely above the steamer, he stayed right with her, scanning the ice and broadcasting minute-by-minute directions. Hour after hour the steamer crawled ahead, "slow as an ant," he says. It was monotonous work for the pilot above and nerve-racking work for the skipper below. Tempers began to run short.

"The Captain says you have him running around in circles!" a despatch from the ship's bridge complained.

"You tell the old man," Jefford barked back, "that I can get him through here, and if he don't like it he can go home!"

At eight in the evening, five hours after the *Columbia* first started through the ice pack, she steamed out, at last, into open sea.

"This is it!" Jefford shouted. "Straight ahead to Nome!"

He flew over her masts and rocked the Vega's wings. The *Columbia* whistled in parting salute as he opened up the engine and headed back to Nome, where the steamer arrived the next day.

"It was no particular feat of navigation," Jefford says of this complicated job of flying. "We could see for twenty miles."

"Big Andy" had more to say about the experience. He knew that even the bush pilots of Alaska feared trips far out over the water in single-engine planes. They shunned the hop to St. Lawrence Island, a matter of only one and a half hours. Jefford, throttling down his engine to low power to save fuel, had cruised above the maze of ice and water seven times as long.

"I took my chance," "Big Andy" says, "and he took his. I

was surprised that he could direct me as well as he did. The boy is tops."

Jefford had enjoyed it, as he enjoys all technical problems. A man of little formal schooling, he has a strong scientific bent which marked his flying almost from the start. Earlier than most of Alaska's bush pilots, he learned the surest way to beat fog and storm. Soon after his arrival in the north he installed a gyro and artificial horizon in his plane, draped a hood around the cockpit and flew blind on some of his mail trips. "It's like playing a fiddle," he told other pilots, most of whom were still flying strictly bush-style. "You must practice and practice."

With Gillam, Jefford was one of the first pilots in Alaska to use instruments. Unlike Gillam, he did not trust long to his own techniques. Five years earlier, he took a trip back to the United States for instruction and earned a full instrument rating. When the C.A.A. arrived in the north to build airways, he went to work for the government because he was keen for the kind of progress that was in the making.

It was dramatic progress. Today thirty-four radio ranges, nine radio beacons and sixty-six weather-reporting and communications stations stand guard on the frosty peaks, the boggy tundra and the gaunt isles of Alaska. Today, for 8,000 miles, the safe, guiding courses of the radio beams criss-cross the northern sky. Instrument landing systems have been installed at major airports. The job of building all this was a staggering one, unlike any that the C.A.A. had ever faced in the United States.

To help lay out the airways, it needed a pilot who knew Alaskan earth and sky conditions. To haul workers and supplies to the remote range and station sites, it needed a pilot of bush freighting ability, for most of these sites were deep in wilderness. To flight-check the new ranges as they went on the air, it needed a pilot adept on instruments. It was lucky to find as versatile a man as Jefford.

The threat of war made the task still bigger. Early in 1941, when most of Alaska lay under snow, the Army asked the C.A.A. if it could also build eleven airfields and have them ready for military use that year. Officers privately doubted that it could be done. It was done. By October, military landings were possible on all eleven. Many men worked hard for this result, but in the opinion of W. L. Seeley, the C.A.A.'s chief engineer, it could not have been done without Jefford.

Seeley believes that Jefford, single-handed, speeded the building of these emergency fields by fifty per cent!

He flew the engineer all over the Far North, and served as far more than a pilot. He personally sifted out half the field and range site possibilities, Seeley says, as they flew along. Landing, he worked as hard on the ground as he had in the air.

He hardly stood on ceremony. Although no one asked him to do so, he helped "walk" the proposed runways. He shoveled snow. When a Diesel engine broke down at one construction camp he rolled up his sleeves and worked over it till he had it running again. One cold night, fearing that a thawing boiler would freeze without attention, he left heated quarters at another camp and stayed beside it till morning in a tent.

Once he and Seeley were circling over a proposed radio range site deep in such rough country that there was no way of landing a plane near it. Seeley suggested that they survey for another site.

"No," drawled Jefford, "that range ought to be right there."

He landed the Cessna in which they were flying on a river bar two miles away. Then, to Seeley's surprise, he pulled a rubber boat from the cabin and began to inflate it. He steered the engineer down two miles of rapids to the site that they had chosen from the air. "He admitted that he had almost no experience as a boatman," Seeley remembers, "but he got me there."

He did all this extra work along with some of the roughest, ruggedest bush flying that has ever been done in the north. He admits that the worst few minutes he ever spent in the air were during one of these war emergency flights with Seeley. Heading toward Anchorage, their plane was caught in a heavy downpour of rain and began to drag toward earth as ice formed on the wings. Jefford managed, by following the dim outline of a small mine railroad, to reach the field at Cordova, where he splashed down on a runway that was covered with an inch of water.

It was still pouring. He waited twenty minutes and then told Seeley that he wanted to take off and make another try for Anchorage.

He climbed high to "top" a mountain range and was flying blind at altitude when ice once more formed on the wings and the ship began to drag dangerously. He dropped to a lower level to shake the ice, found a break in the cloud and hovered low through the driving deluge till he found the mouth of narrow Portage Pass.

The twisting canyon was plugged almost to the ground with fog, but he flew in under it. For a few minutes all went well. He could still see ahead. But as he rounded a right-angle turn he found himself flying blind right in the pass. Wind, at the same time, tossed the Cessna so violently that a second passenger, sitting with his seat belt unfastened, was thrown headlong against the cabin ceiling.

Suddenly the rough face of a glacier seemed to rise up out of flying mists—no more than thirty feet below the plane. Jefford just managed to avoid a crash and fight his way through to the other end of the canyon. "He admitted how close it was," Seeley says. "If he hadn't known that pass like a book, I wouldn't be here now."

As the new radio ranges were built and went on the air Jefford was both able and more than willing to use them. One stormy day two bush pilots flying "contact" along the southeast coast ran out of visibility in a storm and crashed. Jefford, who flew from the States to Alaska, surveying the possibilities of an airway up the coast, fared better.

The storm was no problem to him. He knew that a radio range had been installed at Annette Island, just off the southeast tip of Alaska. Climbing blind to a non-icing level of 7,000 feet, he flew his twin-engine Cessna a routine two and a half hours on instruments and then followed the Annette beam down to a safe landing.

Military pilots arriving in Alaska during the war soon noted that Jefford was a superlative instrument pilot. His skill became a legend, after the airways were in. Time and again, it happened at the fog-drenched Army air base at Nome. The ceiling would be less than 200 feet, visibility less than a quarter of a mile. Long rows of bombers and fighters would be standing motionless along the runways. The airdrome, so far as the Army was concerned, would be closed.

There would be a thunder of engines aloft, traveling back and forth as the pilot overhead made a complicated and carefully timed approach in the narrow space between the radio towers and nearby mountains. Men of the Air Force, looking at the low fog, would shake their heads. "Must be crazy. Or else it's Jefford."

In 1943 the C.A.A. decided to buy a larger plane for Jefford's freighting and patrol work; a DC-3, the transport that was then America's standard airliner. It was a proud day for Jefford. The Douglas looked big indeed on the Far North's frontier airfields. In that year, there was still only one other civilian plane of this size in all Alaska.

He gave the ship a nickname, *King Chris,* and had the title painted with a crown on the side of the nose. But he made no attempt to dress up to his silver airliner. His favorite uniform was still a parka made of rare *sik-sik-puk* skins that he had bought from Archie Ferguson. The headgear he still preferred was a filthy railroad engineer's cap scribbled with numbers and names. The cap did not look out of place as he boarded his official plane, for the ship, like the man, was a workhorse.

In one month, during the construction program, Jefford flew *King Chris* a total of 49,900,000 freight pound-miles, a remarkable record for a DC-3. The plane hauled a 10,000-pound paving machine, in two trips. It hauled the eight-foot frame of a tractor, 6,500-pound Diesel engines and electric generators, TLC radio transmitters broken down. Knocked-down houses, cement, jeeps, tractors, fuel oil, drills, pipe, beacons—almost everything for the airways was by one means or another fitted into *King Chris* and carried through the sky—even a 3,000-foot coil of heavy cable. Jefford and the mechanics had to twist it into a figure eight to cram it inside the fuselage.

Freighting to remote C.A.A. sites, he flew his larger Douglas as another man would fly a Stinson. He landed the wheeled plane fully loaded, in unfavorable winds, on "runways" that would have curled the hair of the engineers who designed it.

Once he set *King Chris* down on top of a bluff at Tin City on an abandoned mine strip 950 feet long. Asked how much of the runway he had used in take-off, he replied, "All of it. I do not plan to go back."

He regularly used small strips like the one at his favorite Eskimo village of Unalakleet, so rough and short that after a small reconnaissance plane nosed over on it the Army closed it to all military aircraft.

To serve a station on St. Lawrence Island, out in the Bering Sea, he landed the airliner in early winter down the snow-covered "main street" of an Eskimo village. There were boat racks on one side, houses on the other, and as he came down the wings nearly grazed them on both sides.

To supply oil for the power-plant of an airways beacon high in the mountains he landed his Douglas each fall on a wild, frozen lake. He had to make the trip late enough for the ice to be solid, yet early enough to avoid deep snow in his plane on wheels. It was a "somewhat tricky job" for a DC-3, he admits. He knew where the lake's springs were, as well as its inlet and its outlet, and avoided these places where the ice might be weak.

Today, with construction virtually complete, Jefford's job has changed. There is less freighting. Flying king of the 8,000-mile airways system, he is ever vigilant for range course displacements which could cause accidents, or for any other fault in the radio aids on which so many pilots depend. To keep airways workers on their toes, he will call the stations from time to time and ask for flight advice. It goes ill for them if their answers are slow or vague. He is unforgiving in his concern for safety.

Although he holds a scheduled airline transport rating, he has turned down airline job offers at twice his government pay. Seldom have a man and a job been so well suited. The work is technical, and all Alaska is Jefford's run. Bush flyers have flown as far and wide, but not as a matter of daily routine.

"We have our own little airline," he once boasted. "We fly everywhere in Alaska and we haul everything on it. If we ever have a uniform, it's going to be the real thing. We'll have hats like MacArthur, boots like the Russians and international-orange pants!"

It is not an easy airline to fly for, even today. When disaster strikes at the remote stations Jefford makes "mercy" flights which are often as dangerous as any he made as a bush pilot. Not long ago two C.A.A. workers were trapped in a blizzard so thick that they lost their way crossing the runway of their own field. The station went off the air. Jefford flew to the dark, abandoned air strip at night, "dragged" it, studying the snow the best he could by the lights of his plane, and brought his ship down in snow so deep that he could not taxi.

Another time, landing at the Annette Island base, he learned from the tower that a plane arriving from the United States, a Norseman, was flying around lost in the neighborhood, trying to land. The pilot, who was in radio contact with the tower, reported that he was "on the south course of the Annette range" but couldn't get over the mountains because the fog was so low.

Jefford, speaking from the tower, told him that there were no mountains on the south course of the range. The pilot agreed that he must indeed be lost. He had only a half hour of fuel left, he reported, and was flying between steep mountain slopes over a stormy sea. Jefford told him to throttle down the engine and wait; he would fly out and try to find him.

Jefford suspected, from his knowledge of the country, that the Norseman was bottled up in one of the forest-fringed inlets of Annette's west course. He shooed all the passengers out of his plane, except one or two who agreed to help him search, and took off, flying low between the water and the low-hanging clouds. It was not long before he sighted the Norseman, just where he had thought it might be. He led the grateful pilot out of the inlet. Then, with the Norseman flying at his wing tip, he entered the overcast, slowing down his plane to the smaller ship's speed, and they landed safely at Annette.

So long as Alaska's airways are maintained by the government Jefford will have an important trouble-shooting job. There are now new instrument landing systems and radar to check. But the main C.A.A. pioneering inside Alaska is over— and he is restless. A few years after the war he took a course in celestial navigation.

"I want to fly the oceans," he explained.

More recently, the one-time bush flyer went to the United States and took a course in jet flying, at an Air Force base in Georgia. He is planning, as a member of the Air National Guard, to fly the Sabre Jets regularly.

"They fascinate me," he says, simply.

Those who know Jefford well wonder whether Alaska itself will hold him much longer. He has flown it as low as fifty feet, and his mind holds a vision of its every jagged peak and twisting river. But now, versatile trail-blazer that he is, he also has another vision of Alaska: long, hard-surfaced runways lying handily near the top of the globe on a natural, short air route between continents.

"There's another kind of pioneering going on today," he says, his eyes keen. "It's being done at altitude. The Arctic is beginning to look like a very small sea."

Chapter *12:* **ALASKA IN THE NEW AIR AGE**

A new kind of pioneer has been making landings and take-offs in Alaska. He is a pilot like Bernt Balchen, the jolly, white-haired Air Force Colonel who left Fairbanks one day in 1949, flew non-stop over the Arctic Ocean to Oslo, then hopped from Oslo to Washington and from Washington back to Fairbanks. Balchen, our leading expert on polar flying, is full of enthusiasm for its future.

"The Arctic," he says, "is in the center of the civilized world."

Another of the new trail-blazers is Charles Blair, the Pan American pilot who landed at Fairbanks in 1951 after a hop over the North Pole from Norway, in a single-engine fighter.

"I decided I wanted to see some new country," Blair casually told reporters. "It was a very simple flight. It's awfully easy to fly over the top of the world."

Today you, too, can fly over the Arctic.

Since 1954, when a Scandinavian airline pioneered the first scheduled trans-Arctic service in history, from California to Denmark, anyone with the price of a ticket can cross the polar sea by air, and the price is going down.

You're likely to find your trans-Arctic journey a lot less adventuresome than a bush flight inside Alaska. You'll see some strange and spectacular sights in the sky, to be sure; in winter, the eerie spokes of northern lights weaving in the darkness about your plane; or in summer the blazing red orb of a midnight sun. You'll look down on an immense sweep of glittering, ice-choked sea that not many human beings have seen before you.

The trip itself, however, will be a routine one. You'll be flying at a high altitude most of the way, sitting comfortably back in a pressurized cabin. The captain up front could tell you that the Arctic route you're flying to Europe is safer and easier than conventional trans-Atlantic route. Weather at altitude is clearer, especially in winter. There is less humidity, less danger of icing. There is much less wind.

The foggy, stormy Arctic weather that took the lives of pioneer pilots in Alaska was low, coastal weather. Flying high over the Arctic in a modern transport is quite different.

Even navigation has been made relatively simple at the top of the world. Your pilot does not face the complex problem which Eielson and Wilkins had to solve for their daring hop in 1928. He is using an American-developed gyro-compass "polar path" system, backed up by celestial navigation. The remarkable new device is linked electrically to his automatic pilot, and it would be difficult for him to lose his way.

We are entering a new air age in which more and more of

the flying between America, Europe and Asia will be over the north.

Today every high school girl and boy knows what Eielson told his round-eyed Fairbanks class long ago: that the shortest routes between the great continents of the northern hemisphere, the air lanes of the future, are the routes which cross or skirt the Arctic Ocean.

You cannot see this clearly on a conventional map. To study the northern hemisphere, you must take a projection centered near the North Pole. Unlike the usual mercator projection, which grossly distorts northern distances, a polar projection shows them as they are, much as you can see them on a globe.

Take a polar projection map, or take a globe, and look down on our last frontier, Alaska. It looks surprisingly central. You will see it ranged with its Canadian, Soviet and Scandinavian neighbors around a rather small ocean. Explorer Stefansson, who foresaw the new air age long before most Americans did, likes to call the Arctic Ocean "the polar Mediterranean."

Today's fast, long-range planes, crossing what Stefansson has called "the shoreless sea of the air," can bring these polar lands and the huge continents that flow down to the south beyond them very close indeed.

Alaska is a pivot land in this new air age. The far-sighted General Billy Mitchell once called it "the most central place in the world of aircraft." The people of Fairbanks like to compare their town to the hub of a wheel, with spokes leading out to the world's great capitals.

Take your globe and stretch a string across it from Fairbanks to these capitals. Measure the distances, and you'll find that

A View of the Globe from Directly Above the North Pole

from Fairbanks it is 3,260 miles to New York, 3,510 to Tokyo, 4,110 to Moscow, 4,210 to London and 4,260 to Berlin!

This does not mean, of course, that most of the world's future international airline routes will cross Alaska. It depends on where you are flying from and where you are going. The Great Circle routes between most of the United States and Europe cross over Canada and the Greenland region. Alaska lies on the Great Circle routes between most of the United States and the Orient. Since 1949, Northwest Airlines has been making scheduled flights through Alaska to Tokyo.

The short, Great Circle route from Moscow to the West Coast of the United States is over the polar sea, and crosses the sky close to Alaska. As long ago as 1937 a Soviet pilot made a pioneer flight along this route, landing in California. The Russians developed extensive flying out over the Arctic Ocean long before we did.

Our new jet transports could fly the polar route from Fairbanks to Moscow, or vice versa, in some seven and a half hours. Tomorrow's jet transports, which experts predict will cruise at a thousand miles an hour at an altitude of 50,000 to 60,000 feet, could make the trip in some four hours!

America's Arctic flying has probably tripled, in the years since the war. Most of it has been military. Cooperating with Canada and Denmark, we have built an "early-warning" radar network across the north, and a chain of bases and weather and refueling stations stretches all the way from Alaska to Greenland.

Another new air pioneer in the north is Lt. Col. Joseph O. Fletcher, of Shawnee, Oklahoma. In March, 1952 he landed a ski-equipped Air Force plane on a floating ice island 115 miles from the North Pole, and established a semi-permanent weather station on it. Two months later he was co-pilot of the first Air Force plane to land at the Pole itself.

Polar flying is now routine for our military pilots. Since 1947, a weather reconnaissance squadron stationed at Eielson Air Force Base, near Fairbanks, has been making regular flights to or close to the Pole. By late 1955 the squadron had flown 1600 such missions.

"If there is a third world war," General Henry H. Arnold said, "the strategic center of it will be the North Pole."

It is a terrifying and challenging age in which Alaska has become a pivot land. No one can foretell the future of flight through Alaska without knowing whether we are to have war or peace; and if it is peace, whether reciprocal airline routes may one day be opened between the United States and the Soviet Union and Red China. If this should happen, Alaska would become a great thoroughfare of trade and travel, truly a crossroads of the world.

*

Within the borders of Alaska, the progress of aviation continues to be rapid. In 1955 there were 1400 planes based there, nearly ten times as many as there were just before the war. Ten times as much freight was being hauled by air, and there were seven times as many passengers, not including traffic to and from the United States. The flyingest people under the American flag are still setting new records.

While much of the mainline flying is now being done along the airways in larger, multi-engine planes, small planes, manned by a new fraternity of young bush pilots, are still the mainstay of the hinterland.

Bush pilots are still pioneering, in this huge frontier country whose rich resources have only begun to be tapped. Wherever there is exploring, for oil, for uranium, for copper, for tin, for manganese, bush pilots are coming down to land in the wilds.

Today, as more and more Americans from the States are discovering Alaska, airlines founded by men like Noel Wien and Bob Reeve are also helping to pioneer an important tourist business. They are speeding visitors to Eskimoland, at the top of the continent, and to other remote places like the fur-seal islands of the Bering Sea.

Today you cross the wilderness with a bush pilot in his single-engine ship, maybe a Norseman or a Cessna. You watch him weave his way under fog, dodge on top, spiral down through a hole and break out into sunshine beyond. He lands at a small Arctic strip and starts to unload the freight as a crowd of welcoming people stand around.

All at once there is a rending scream in the sky.

It's an Air Force jet that is streaking high above you, heading on a routine hop toward the North Pole. It's traveling fast, almost as fast as sound, leaving a long, white vapor trail in the blue sky.

You wonder about the uniformed pilot up there with his complicated instrument panels, rushing toward the top of the world as the rough-clad pilot beside you prepares to take off again over the hills, flying slowly by the lay of the land.

"All in the day's work," you think. That is what both men would say.

You stand there on the runway where a small wind sock flaps in the breeze and you look up to see the jet's white vapor trail drifting away into the "shoreless sea of the air."

You are full of awe; for the great pioneering of yesterday and today, and for the polar age of tomorrow in which Alaska will play so important a part.

C.A.A.

Arctic
Barrow
Wainwright
North Cape
SIBERIA
Amguema
70°
Point Lay
Meade
Point Hope
Brooks
Noatak
East Cape
Diomede Is.
Kotzebue
Kiana
Kobuk
Shungnak
Noorvik
Selawik
Bering Strait
Wales
Teller
Seward Pen.
Koyukuk
65°
Gambell
St. Lawrence I.
Nome
U.S.S.R.
U.S.
Ruby
Unalakleet
Bering
Nowitna
Ophir
Takotna
McGrath
Iditarod
Flat
Yukon
Kuskokwim
Nyak
Bethel
60°
Sea
Dillingham
Pribilof Is.
Alaska Peninsula
Kodiak
170°W
55°N
165°
160°
155°
Aleutian Is.
Dutch Harbor
Cold Bay
Unimak I.
Umnak I.
Unalaska I.